ENGLISH GARDEN
ORNAMENT

English Garden Ornament

By Paul Edwards

South Brunswick and New York: A. S. Barnes and Company

Library of Congress Catalogue Card Number: **67-13083**

A. S. Barnes and Co., Inc.
Cranbury, New Jersey 08512

6598

Printed in the United States of America

TO JANE AND JULIAN

ACKNOWLEDGEMENTS

MY thanks for help in the preparation of this book are due to my friend Mr. J. C. Brown, architect and designer of the horse-decorated seats at the Belgrade Theatre Square, Coventry; to Mr. Walter Ritchie, sculptor; to Mr. John Holliday, until recently the Senior Lecturer at the Birmingham School of Planning and Landscape Architecture; to Mr. John Bridgeman, sculptor, and the designer of many pieces of play sculpture in Birmingham; to Mr. C. A. Scott, Museums Curator, and Mrs. Charmian Woodfield, archaeologist, of the Herbert Art Gallery and Museum, Coventry; to Messrs. Boulton and Paul Ltd. and Mr. J. D. Paul of that Company who kindly supplied photographic copies of their 1896 catalogue; to The Bo'ness Iron Co. Ltd. for supplying a copy of their 1928 catalogue; to Miss Gillian Aston, who typed much of the manuscript; and finally to my family who have encouraged and accompanied me on countless visits to parks and gardens in Britain.

PREFACE

THIS book is an attempt to describe the wide variety of ornament that has been made for gardens and parks, and to relate this ornament to the aesthetic and social changes that have affected the English garden. Some of the ornament, notably garden buildings, sculpture, and ironwork, are very fine works of art in their own right and deserve to be better known and sometimes more cherished. Often pieces of garden ornament are all that survives from an earlier layout or were intimately connected with a past mode of living.

During recent years there has been a growing interest in the great gardens of Britain, and each year sees an increasing number of people visiting these gardens which are now nearly all open to the public at some time of the year, by the National Trust, or under the National Gardens Scheme, or privately.

Some appreciation of the history and styles of gardening and landscape design together with a knowledge of garden plants will obviously greatly add to the pleasures to be enjoyed by visitors to these beautiful parks and gardens. There are many books—and each year sees further publications—on the history of the English garden, or describing the wealth of garden plants cultivated in Britain, but little information is available on the man-made objects such as decorative garden buildings and furniture, sculptured ornaments, and other features that contribute so much to a good garden design.

Sometimes the care and maintenance of ornaments in our gardens and public parks is largely ignored and although many garden buildings are now being restored, often with financial aid from the government, many are still ill kept. Decorative ironwork for example is sometimes unpainted and rusting is allowed to go on unchecked. When fine features and ornaments are ignored and neglected, the garden is in danger of losing works of art and craftsmanship which are often irreplaceable.

The author would like to hope that this book may promote a greater awareness of our heritage of garden ornament which in turn should help to ensure their necessary maintenance and therefore survival, and at the same time to encourage better standards in contemporary garden decoration.

CONTENTS

THE PLATES

COLOR PLATES

MONOCHROME

1. 17th-century gazebo, Packwood House, Warwickshire
2. 17th-century pigeon house, Rousham, Oxfordshire
3. Orangery and conservatory, Woburn Abbey, Bedfordshire
4. Conservatory in the Hindoo Gothic Style, Sezincote, Gloucestershire
5. 18th-century garden pavilion, Farnborough Hall, Warwickshire
6. Palladian bridge, Stowe, Buckinghamshire
7. Chinese pagoda, Woburn Abbey, Bedfordshire
8. Grotto in the conservatory, Rousham, Oxfordshire
9. Early 19th-century summer-house, Charlecote, Warwickshire
10. Wrought iron garden chair, Hidcote Manor, Gloucestershire
11. Wrought iron garden chairs, Lanhydrock House, Cornwall
12. Wrought iron seat, Packwood House, Warwickshire
13. Wrought iron seat, Charlecote, Warwickshire
14. Cast iron seat, Hidcote Manor, Gloucestershire
15. Cast iron seat with fern frond pattern, Lanhydrock, Cornwall
16. A Furness Railway seat in author's garden
17. Armillary sundial, Woburn Abbey, Bedfordshire
18. Scheemakers' Dying Gladiator, Rousham, Oxfordshire
19. 18th-century lead figure of a shepherd, Charlecote, Warwickshire
20. Stone urn, Woburn Abbey, Bedfordshire
21. Bronze urn modelled by Louis Ballin, goldsmith to Louis XIV, Lanhydrock House, Cornwall
22. Lead figures of deer in the wild garden, Batsford Park, Gloucestershire
23. Figure in concrete in author's garden. Sculptor, John Bridgeman
24. Stone Japanese lantern, Batsford Park, Gloucestershire
25. Children's play sculpture, Rhambshov Park, Stockholm
26. Children's play sculpture, Rhambshov Park, Stockholm
27. Topiary chessmen, Compton Wynyates, Warwickshire
28. Topiary figure of a Beefeater, Compton Wynyates, Warwickshire
29. Topiary figure of a cat, Compton Wynyates, Warwickshire
30. Children's log maze, Birmingham Parks Department
31. Cold bath, Packwood House, Warwickshire
32. Lead fountain wall mask, Packwood House, Warwickshire
33. Cast iron pump, Chipping Campden, Gloucestershire
34. The grotto, Woburn Abbey, Bedfordshire
35. 17th-century gatehouse, Lanhydrock House, Cornwall
36. Entrance gates and gate piers, Charlecote Park, Warwickshire
37. Early 18th-century gateway with wrought iron overthrow, Packwood House, Warwickshire
38. 19th-century gate lodge, Batsford Park, Gloucestershire
39. Timber entrance gates with Cotswold stone gate piers
40. Timber gallery, New Place, Stratford upon Avon

THE DRAWINGS

ENGLISH GARDEN
ORNAMENT

1. 17th-century gazebo, Packwood House, Warwickshire

Chapter One

GARDEN BUILDINGS

Gazebos; dovecotes and pigeon houses; orangeries and conservatories; garden temples, pavilions, bridges, etc.; Chinese, Indian and Gothic styles; ruins, follies, and grottoes; root houses and hermits' huts; ice-houses; summer-houses.

SINCE the time when Adam and Eve left the Garden of Eden, man has come not only to cultivate his garden but also to adorn it. From Tudor times to the present day an immensely interesting variety of buildings has been constructed to decorate the English garden and park. Some of the buildings are gems of architecture, such as the temples and pavilions designed in the 18th century or the Regency period, whilst the complete range makes a fascinating pictorial history of the development of our taste for landscape.

Our early gardens, like the large houses they surrounded, always afforded some defence against intruders and therefore were essentially places of seclusion. The usual form of defence was a substantial wall which kept out not only wild beasts and wild men but also views of the outside world. As the countryside became tamed and contained fewer terrors for man so the desire grew to look outwards from the garden. It was to meet this wish that the enclosing garden wall, usually at a corner, was developed to form a covered room or gazebo, as they were later called, where members of the household—in particular the women and children —could view the wider landscape.

The best surviving example of a Tudor gazebo is the one at Melford Hall, Suffolk (Fig. 1). It was built in about 1560 and has recently been restored by the National Trust, who now own the property. The building is octagonal in plan and has attractive brick finials projecting upwards from each gable and corner shaft. Packwood House, Warwickshire, is particularly well supplied with gazebos, for there is one in each of the four corners of the walled Carolean garden. The one in the south-east corner (Plate 1) was built in the 17th century, and the decorative wrought ironwork and trained vine add greatly to the attractiveness of this charming garden building. The less decorated gazebo in the south-west corner terminates the terrace walk that runs between the Carolean garden and the famous Yew Garden, and so commands good views of both gardens.

The fashion for building gazebos returned in the 19th and early 20th centuries when formal layouts and enclosing garden walls were once again in vogue. Many of these later gazebos were sited to give the occupant a view of some fine scenery or of passing traffic—before, of course, the internal combustion engine made this less of a novelty.

Besides giving a view of the outside world, Tudor garden houses were also sited to provide a pleasing prospect of the cultivated grounds about the house. These garden buildings would normally be connected to the house by a raised terrace,

FIG. 1.   Tudor gazebo, Melford Hall, Suffolk

also reflected in their materials of construction, such as the stone pigeon houses of Northumberland, or the red brick ones in East Anglia.   By the end of the 17th century an octagonal or circular plan, with a domed roof surmounted by a small cupola with openings for the pigeons, was more usual.   The interior walls would be lined with a vast number of pigeon holes and nests. Access to the pigeon holes would be obtained from a ladder suspended from a beam which in turn was attached to a revolving column.   The pigeon house at Rousham, Oxfordshire (Plate 2), dated 1685, still contains its original fittings and is a delightful

FIG. 2.   Chinese pagoda, Royal Botanic Gardens, Kew

which was a popular feature of the Tudor garden, as it afforded an elevated position for seeing and appreciating the intricate patterns of the knot and parterre gardens of the time.   Tudor garden houses were often built to provide very good protection against the weather and would sometimes be equipped with a chimney and fireplace.

Another and more indispensable building to be found in the grounds of most manor houses was the columbarium, or pigeon house.   Domestic cattle were then killed at Michaelmas and salted down for later use throughout the winter.   Fresh meat during the winter was therefore a rare delicacy.   Fledgling pigeons or squabs fresh from the columbarium provided a very welcome delicacy for any table.   In Tudor times the keeping of pigeons was especially popular, and even the poor had lofts containing a few breeding pairs.   Eventually the birds were bred in such great numbers that their heavy feeding on other men's fields led to their disrepute, and the decline in pigeon rearing.

Before the 16th century, pigeon houses and dovecotes were usually built in daub and wattle, but later were more important features of the garden.   In Tudor times large columbaria were constructed to yield a supply of up to 3,000 pigeons a year for the lord of the manor's table.   Tudor pigeon houses were usually designed with a square plan and with gabled walls.   Locality is

centre-piece to the formal gardens.   Smaller dovecotes would be simpler but just as elegant in design and might be built as a part of the garden wall or at the top of a free-standing column.   Long after their usefulness had passed in providing a welcome addition to the restricted diet of the times, dovecotes were still used by garden designers as an interesting feature in a formal garden layout.   In the latter half of the 18th century the design of garden aviaries became more fanciful and the Chinese style of ornament was often used to decorate these structures.   Sir William Chambers (1726-1796) did much to popularise the Chinese style of decoration for garden buildings, and built in the grounds of the Royal Gardens at Kew (now the Royal Botanic

2. 17th-century pigeon house, Rousham, Oxfordshire

Gardens) an aviary, a pagoda, which is still there (Fig. 2), and a bridge, all in the Chinese manner. The Chinese style extended itself in the hands of imaginative designers to such whimsical but pleasing garden buildings as the Chinese Dairy at Woburn Abbey, Bedfordshire, where there is also a small timber pagoda (Plate 7), forming a delightful central feature in the maze. The most exquisite pagoda of all was built at Alton Towers, Staffordshire, in the late 1820's (Frontispiece & Fig. 3). It is sited on an island in one of the lower ponds at the bottom of the valley. It is three storeys high but was originally planned to have six with a

FIG. 3.   Chinese pagoda, Alton Towers, Staffordshire

small gasholder at the ground floor to supply the many gaslit Chinese lamps above. Figures of Chinese monsters were to have further decorated the building and to have spouted water from their eyes, nostrils, fins and tails, and a column of water was to have shot forth some seventy feet into the air from the top of the pagoda. However, the design that was eventually carried out, and which can be seen today, was a much more simple and graceful composition. The lattice-like wall of cast iron forming the circular core of the pagoda is particularly attractive.

The orangery was another building that was first introduced into the garden for a utilitarian purpose, but which later became of such visual importance that some of the best designers were commissioned to prepare drawings for their construction (Plate 3). The utilitarian function of the orangery was to provide housing

during the winter months for the tubs of orange, lemon and lime trees that were displayed during the summer in the formal gardens adjoining the house. The fashion for growing orange trees in this way goes back to some of the earliest Italian villa gardens. In 17th-century England, most large houses had their orangery, and the vogue continued well into the 19th century.

In 1704 the beautiful orangery at Kensington Palace was built by Sir Christopher Wren, and from then on throughout the 18th century the leading architects of the day, in particular Robert Adam, Henry Holland and the landscape architect Capability Brown, were to be commissioned to design orangeries. The style in which they were built was invariably classical with the satisfying simplicity and good proportions one associates with Georgian buildings. Protection from the inclement winter weather and the provision of heating was of course known to be needed, but light during the short days of winter was not thought to be particularly important for the plants. In fact it was not until the 19th century that adequate light was understood to be essential to the plants' health, and it was only then that top-lighting was introduced into the design of conservatories. It was the Regency landscape architect Humphry Repton who first recognised the value of putting top-lighting into conservatories and glasshouses. Once this was recognised many earlier orangeries had their original roof replaced by glass, but hidden from view by a parapet wall. Repton also helped to develop the orangery, or winter garden as he called it, into a more integral part of the house rather than as a separate building.

The winter garden or conservatory soon became popular with those who could afford it in Victorian England. The rapid growth of the merchant middle classes around most of our cities produced a popular demand for miniature estates and any innovation such as a conservatory was quickly accepted and soon became an almost indispensable part of the Victorian and Edwardian villa. The popularity of the conservatory naturally increased the interest in the rapidly widening range of exotic plants that could be grown successfully under glass. Most Victorian gardening books give a fascinating range of these plants, not forgetting that great favourite, the beautiful Tea Rose. The Tea Rose got its name from its scent which resembled that of China tea chests which were imported into Britain at that time. They were exquisite roses, but unfortunately not hardy enough for general cultivation out of doors in Britain. In the new conservatories they flourished to perfection and became a firm favourite during the latter half of the 19th century. The white 'Niphetos', the pale rose 'Madame Cochet', or the yellow 'Madame Hoste' were then household words with endearing associations.

The conservatory, besides becoming a part of the middle-class domestic scene, also helped to link the formality of the house with the irregularity and variety of the garden. Regency architects and landscape architects were greatly concerned with the linking of the house with the garden. In the 18th-century landscape park, only the inconspicuous ha-ha or sunk fence was provided to mark the extent of the home grounds around the house and to give protection to members of the household from the cattle or deer in the park. Humphry Repton (1752-1838), a leading figure in Regency architecture and landscape design, was concerned with 'dressing' these home grounds for the convenience of the members of the household and linking the house with the garden. The restoration of the terrace helped in this desired link, as also did the use of the french window, balcony, verandah and conservatory. At Sezincote, Gloucestershire, where the architect Samuel Pepys Cockerell and Thomas Daniell were pioneering the use of the Hindoo Gothic style of architecture and Humphry Repton was giving advice on the layout of the grounds in the early 19th century, a beautiful curving conservatory embraces a part of the garden and provides the desired link between the living rooms and the landscape (Plate 4). The growing interest in conservatories led to new materials being used in their construction, both for cheapness and to give the maximum amount of glass and therefore light for the plants. Under that great land-

3. Orangery and conservatory, Woburn Abbey, Bedfordshire

scape architect Sir Joseph Paxton (1803-1865) the use of cast iron and prefabrication in the construction of large glasshouses and conservatories led to the building of one of the engineering wonders of the Victorian era, the 1851 Great Exhibition building, better known as the Crystal Palace when it was moved and enlarged at its more permanent home at Sydenham. The Great Exhibition building measured 1,848 feet long by 450 feet broad, and was 66 feet high. It was built in the incredibly short time of seventeen weeks, a speed of erection that could only have been achieved by prefabrication. The transept enclosed a group of large elm trees. Previous proposals for the Exhibition building if carried out would have meant the felling of these trees, and the public had not taken kindly to this possibility. When the building was re-erected and enlarged at Sydenham it covered no less than eighteen acres. In under forty years the winter garden had developed from housing exotic plants to housing the greatest industrial exhibition the world had so far seen—such was the pace of change in the new industrial Britain.

The influence of the formal style of the French Renaissance on the design of parks and gardens in England during the 17th century brought about a new attitude to garden buildings and ornament, for in the Renaissance garden, buildings were designed primarily to be seen in a composed setting rather than for the view that might be obtained from them. To begin with they were built in the classical manner. Sometimes they were on such a palatial scale that they were also used as banqueting houses. The architect Sir John Vanbrugh (1664-1726) built an imposing Banqueting House at Castle Howard, Yorkshire in 1700, and a pavilion built by Thomas Archer between 1709 and 1711 at Wrest, Bedfordshire was on a similar scale. In this formal style of gardening the classical garden house was sited at the end of a tree-lined vista, but with the Picturesque Landscape Movement which started in the 1730's the layout of parks and estates became more irregular but respectful of the natural genius of the site. No longer was everything symmetrical or the ground levelled and terraced, the trees planted in rows and avenues or the water contained in canals and basins of geometric shapes. The picturesque style was a marriage of art and nature; an English compromise, so apt and so suited to our climate and countryside. 'Nature abhors a straight line' and prefers the gentle curving line of stream, lake, woodland, or land form, claimed the 18th-century landscape theorist. The theories were rapidly put into practice in the landscaping of gardens, parks, and estate farmlands which contributed so much to the creation in lowland Britain of our typical and much loved England countryside. It accepted

our rolling topography, our moist climate, and allowed gardening, farming, and forestry to be practised to the benefit of each other.

Buildings in this landscape would, if well designed and sited, enliven a scene and provide by their contrast to natural forms, a focal point in the composition. Most of these garden buildings in the first half of the 18th century were designed in the classical style as temples or pavilions. They were usually either circular or oval in plan, built of stone with columns and perhaps pilasters, and having a domed roof; or rectangular in plan with a portico front, and a pedimented roof. The word 'pavilion' in France was used to describe a miniature palace that was built in the royal garden or park to house the mistresses of the court. They were invariably delightful pieces of architecture built with none of the pretentiousness of the royal palace. The size of these French pavilions usually made them perfectly in scale with the garden, and they were looked upon as an important part of a grand garden design. In England they rarely housed a mistress, but instead were used for more innocent pleasures such as banquets or simple picnics. The word 'temple' is mostly reserved for smaller garden buildings that would provide a seat or house a statue of a Greek god or goddess, to which the temple would be dedicated. As with pavilions, the French often had a more practical use in mind when building garden temples. Instead of designing the temple as a visual attraction in the landscape, as would be the case in England, the French garden designer had to site the *Temples d'Amour* in some hidden part of the garden so that lovers might make good use of this convenient and romantic shelter.

At Farnborough Hall, Warwickshire, there is a charming 18th-century oval pavilion (Plate 5). It is built of stone and has a portico on the ground floor which supports an upper storey room, reached by a curved flight of steps at the rear of the pavilion. The interior decoration has recently been restored, including the delightful but restrained plasterwork, so that visitors to this National Trust property at Farnborough can now fully appreciate the charm of an 18th-century garden pavilion in all its exquisite and original detail.

It was also in the Renaissance garden in 17th-century England that bridges became important ornamental features in the landscape. With the picturesque park are associated some of our most beautiful bridges. The most notable and most purely ornamental bridge from this period is the Palladian bridge which was first built at Wilton House, Wiltshire, by the ninth Earl of Pembroke with the professional assistance of Robert Morris, in 1737. As the name indicates, the design of the bridge was adapted

4. Conservatory in the Hindoo Gothic Style, Sezincote, Gloucestershire

from designs of the 16th-century Italian architect Andrea Palladio, whose work was to have such an important influence on Georgian architects, notably William Kent and Robert Adam. Further Palladian bridges were built at Stowe, Buckinghamshire (Plate 6) and at Prior Park, near Bath. Their design was very grandiose

FIG. 4.   Robert Adam's bridge, at Compton Verney, Warwickshire

but very effective in terminating a view such as the long sweeping valley at Prior Park. The Palladian bridge consisted of several arches with the main span centrally placed, surmounted by balustrades and pillars carrying a pedimented roof and decorated ceiling.

Larger and less purely ornamental bridges were built: by Sir John Vanbrugh at Blenheim, one of which was later partly submerged by Capability Brown's improvements to the water; by Robert Adam at Kedleston, Derbyshire, and at Compton Verney, Warwickshire (1761–5) (Fig. 4); by James Paine at Chatsworth, Derbyshire; and by James Wyatt at Chiswick. This fine tradition of stone bridges in the park and garden continued until the time of Sir John Soane, whose bridge at Tyringham, Buckinghamshire, built in 1795, is one of his finest architectural works.

On a less monumental scale were the Chinese bridges, built either in stone or timber in parks and gardens in the 18th century. Sir William Chambers' writings on Chinese gardens and buildings did much to popularise the Chinese taste in England at this time, as did W. Wrighte's book *Grotesque Architecture* (1767) and A. Wallis's book *The Carpenter's Treasure* (1773), both of which contained drawings of Chinese bridges which could be easily constructed by estate craftsmen. The Chinese style for garden bridges continued to be popular well into the 19th century. A fine Chinese bridge was constructed in stone across Capability Brown's serpentined water at Wrest Park, Bedfordshire as late as 1874 (Fig. 5).

5.   18th-century garden pavilion, Farnborough Hall, Warwickshire

Fig. 5. Chinese bridge, Wrest Park, Bedfordshire

The most famous garden layout in the first half of the 18th century was undoubtedly at Lord Cobham's seat at Stowe, Buckinghamshire, now a public school. The gardens were first laid out by Sir John Vanbrugh and the garden designer Charles Bridgeman in 1713. The layout was then more or less formal in style, with garden buildings designed by Vanbrugh, such as the Rotunda, the Pyramid and the Temple of Bacchus (now demolished), axially placed at the end of formal vistas. The rotunda was erected in *c.* 1719 and then contained a statue of Venus. By 1763 the building had been altered by G. B. Borra who redesigned the dome, entablature and capitals. William Kent (1685-1748) was later called in to make further improvements to the four hundred acres of park and garden. Kent's landscaping rubbed out most of the formality from the original design, so that the octagonal lake and the canal became more natural-looking stretches of water, and the parkland was composed of open glades and grouped trees and woodland. Kent worked on various garden buildings at Stowe until his death in 1748. These include the Temple of Ancient Virtue (the temple to Modern Virtue was built as a ruin), the Queen's Building, Congreve's Monument, the Temple of Concord and Victory (based on the Maison Carrée at Nîmes and completed by Borra), the Palladian Bridge, the Temple of Venus (a popular dedication in the 18th century), the Temple of British Worthies, the South Doric Pavilions (altered by Borra), and the Hermitage. The

architect of the Radcliffe Camera Library at Oxford, James Gibbs (1682-1754), designed and had built at Stowe the Boycott Pavilions, Lord Cobham's Pillar, and the Gothic Temple. But these, however, were only the main ornaments in the grounds. A walk or ride in the park would disclose equestrian statues, grottoes, alcoves, a witch's house, obelisks, inscriptions and monuments to such national figures and heroes as General Wolfe, Captain Cook, Captain Grenville, Congreve, and Queen Caroline.

Lord Cobham's mania for garden decoration at Stowe continued until his death in 1749, when he was succeeded by his nephew Earl Temple who, besides having such an appropriate title, added yet more ornaments to the grounds. Stowe during this time became as famous and as much visited as Versailles and contributed more than any other garden to the new fashion on the Continent for the '*Jardin Anglais*'.

Many present-day writers on gardens describe Stourhead in Wiltshire as the greatest 18th-century landscape garden, but it would be more accurate to describe it as one of the best-kept examples. Unfortunately Stowe is neglected and largely ignored. Kent's delightful Temple to Ancient Virtue, for example, is sprouting sapling trees from its dome, and whilst a ruinous state may be historically more accurate, aesthetically the neglect will become disastrous. Many other garden buildings and ornaments at Stowe are in need of careful restoration and maintenance, together with the lakes, 'rivers' and rills, paths and lawns which are choked or overgrown with weeds. The Ministry of Works are now starting to help to repair the temples and ornaments and it is to be hoped that all the buildings will be soon out of the danger of becoming unintentional ruins. If ways can be found completely to restore and properly maintain these historic and still beautiful gardens, Stowe would again rank as highly, and give as much enjoyment, as any other 18th-century landscape garden still existing in this country. When one considers that the invention of the landscape garden in the 18th century was one of this country's best contributions to Western architecture it is to be hoped that ways and means will be found to restore and once again cherish the historic grounds at Stowe.

Social life at many of the country seats in Restoration England during much of the 18th century was boisterous and high-spirited to say the least. It is not therefore surprising to find one contemporary writer saying that the gardens at Stowe give 'free scope to inclinations of every kind, and if in some parts they humour the sensualist's debauched taste, in others they pay very noble compliments to virtue'. At West Wycombe in the 1760's, Sir Francis Dashwood, second baronet (afterwards Lord le

Despencer), took the 'sensualist's debauched taste' to even further lengths when he is supposed to have modelled a part of his garden in the shape of a woman's body, and to have built, according to John Wilkes, a 'lewd temple dedicated to Tristram Shandy's "Tetragrammaton".'[1]

Sir Francis Dashwood had succeeded to the seat at West Wycombe at the age of sixteen, in 1724. From that time onwards he was the centre of rumour and notoriety. As a young man when taking the Grand Tour and visiting most of the courts of Europe, he was said to have masqueraded as Charles XII of Sweden and aspired to be the lover of Tsarina Anne. Whilst in Rome during Holy Week he obtained admission to scourging ceremonies in the Sistine Chapel, and when the lights were extinguished and the flagellations began, he brought out his riding whip with which he joined in the flagellation in no uncertain manner until the congregation were crying out 'Il Diavolo'. In fairness it must be said that Sir Francis was also a

man of much learning and a keen follower and patron of the arts. 'Grecian Taste and Roman Spirit' perhaps best summed up the attitude to life of many 18th-century noblemen, and this in fact was one of the toasts of the Dilettanti Society, a society Sir Francis helped to form. His fondness for pranks and eccentricities resulted in his playing a leading part in forming the now notorious Hell Fire Club, whose members were known as the Monks of Medmenham. Originally, there were twelve members, mostly friends of Frederick, Prince of Wales, and these twelve included such figures as Lord Sandwich and the notorious Bubb Dodington, who in his younger days had built the enormous house and formal gardens at Eastbury, Dorsetshire. Sir Francis Dashwood took a lease of Medmenham Abbey, which then consisted of a ruined church and some acres of land situated a few miles from West Wycombe, and there set up the weird meeting place for the 'monks'. Every type of imaginable orgy was reputed to have taken place and certainly from contemporary descriptions of the buildings and gardens one is led to believe that this was the primary occupation of the 'Monks of Medmenham' or as they were sometimes called the 'Knights of St. Francis of

[1] *The Life and Opinions of Tristram Shandy, Gentleman,* by Laurence Sterne, published in nine volumes from 1759 to 1766.

6.   Palladian bridge, Stowe, Buckinghamshire

Wycombe'. The garden, the grove, the orchard, the neighbouring woods, all spoke of the loves and frailties of the younger monks, who seem at least to have sinned naturally,' wrote Wilkes.

When Bubb Dodington (by then Baron Melcombe) died he left £500 for his ashes to be housed in a temple at West Wycombe. Sir Francis had the temple built adjoining the village church which in time became something of a mausoleum for many of the 'Knights of St. Francis of Wycombe'. The mausoleum is hexagonal in plan, open in the centre, and the walls are faced with flint with niches for urns, and arches and windows are provided for viewing the surrounding landscape. The village church was also largely rebuilt by Sir Francis. The tower was crowned by a large ball, large enough to hold ten or a dozen people. Many travellers by rail on the Great Western line must have wondered why this glinting golden ball was built over the church tower at West Wycombe. The reason seems uncertain but, as might be guessed, such a folly built by Sir Francis has given rise to many stories as to what actually went on in this lofty hide-out. But the church and the mausoleum were also sited and built to form an important part of the carefully contrived parkland that formed such an essential feature of an 18th-century seat, even if as Wilkes said the 'village church was built on the top of the hill for the convenience and devotion of the town at the bottom of it'.

In 1800, Humphry Repton was called in to make recommendations on the layout of the grounds at West Wycombe, and was most impressed by much of the park and in particular the lake which had been formed by damming the diminutive river Wye. Today the lake with less water is less dramatic, for once a completely rigged ship floated there, 'her masts rising above the adjoining trees in a manner which adds greatly to the landscape', wrote Arthur Young when he saw the grounds in 1767. Whereas the ship has not survived, a number of graceful temples remain. On the island in the lake there is the white Temple of Music, and in the park the temples to Flora and Daphne, and the Temple to the Four Winds, whilst near the south colonnade of the house there is a curious Tuscan archway built in flint with a cock loft over the arch. West Wycombe also has its cave or grotto which was dug into the hillside to the south of the church and mausoleum in about 1750, and which had a room at the end of the tunnel for alleged meetings of the Hell Fire Club. The cave can still be seen.

Whilst buildings and follies associated with Hell Fire Clubs were of course the exception rather than the rule in 18th-century England, nevertheless different types of garden ornament were now being associated with different emotions. Moods of grandeur, melancholy, beauty, or the sublime were now expected to enliven the walk around the picturesque garden. The buildings and other ornaments, from grandiose temples to Gothic ruins or watery grottoes, could greatly help to promote the right emotions for a particular part of the garden. The 18th-century landowner expected to enjoy from his stroll around his domain a variety of emotional sensations that are now more usually provided by a wide range of modern inventions, such as radio, films, television, motor-cars, and of course the greatly increased number of sports.

The association of different emotions with different objects, arose from the new experience of feeling through the senses, rather than from the old appeal of the Renaissance garden which relied on mathematical perfection. It was about this time that Edmund Burke, a keen follower of the landscape movement, wrote his important work on the subject of aesthetics which was published in 1757, entitled *Inquiry into the Origin of Our Ideas of the Sublime and Beautiful*. In this book Burke classified objects of beauty, and attributed their beauty to roundness and smoothness. This association with rounded forms was, Burke believed, derived from feminine beauty. The sublime was shown to be a compound of beauty and horror emotion, such as was felt from darkness, ruggedness, and vastness. A mixture of the beautiful and the sublime was harmonised by Claude Lorraine in his landscape paintings. Claude was the first European painter of landscapes; previously if landscape was shown at all it was as a background to a figure or portrait painting. His paintings and drawings were highly thought of in this country, and many English noblemen when taking the Grand Tour through France and Italy brought back with them a Claude painting or drawing. Many of these compositions gave direct inspiration to the makers of picturesque scenery in England, notably at Pains Hill, Surrey, and at Bowood, Wiltshire, both by that pioneer amateur landscapist the Hon. Charles Hamilton. Most of Claude's landscapes depicted smooth scenery with the contrasting sublimity coming from ruins, cascades or even a hermitage, placed usually in the middle distance.

Rounded forms and the curving line of beauty was of course the underlying principle of all of Capability Brown's landscape work, whether he was designing lakes, woods, clumps of trees, undulating lawns, or entrance drives.

The strong taste for the sublime in England during the 18th century led to the 'horrid gloom' and fantasy of grottoes and the building of 'ancient ruins', Gothic ornamentation as first seen in garden buildings, and inscriptions on urns and pillars to give the right sort of associations with moods of melancholy, sublimity, or the heroic past.

With the greater interest in, and the desire to enjoy a variety of emotions from garden scenes, it is not surprising that later 18th-century and Regency designers should turn to styles other than classical for the building of garden temples and pavilions. After Horace Walpole's experiments at Strawberry Hill, Twickenham, Gothic became a popular style for many garden buildings, and soon more exotic styles such as Chinese and Indian were adopted.

Indian decoration became particularly popular in the Regency period. It was first promoted by the landscape painter Thomas Daniell, who, with his nephew William Daniell, had spent ten years travelling and painting in India, and on his return to England prepared and published, in 1801, his famous book *Oriental Scenery*. This book, with its 144 views of oriental landscape and decoration, together with the growing interest in Indian art from the increasing number of people who had worked in India, soon promoted a minor craze for Indian decoration. The house and conservatory at Sezincote, Gloucestershire (see also page 19) which was designed in the Hindoo Gothic style in the early 19th century by Samuel Pepys Cockerell,[1] was directly inspired by Daniell's sketches of Indian decoration. Samuel Pepys Cockerell was brother of the owner of Sezincote, Sir Charles Cockerell, M.P. Both had connections with the East India Company; Samuel being for some time the Surveyor to East India House. The garden at Sezincote was laid out by Humphry Repton and Daniell, the latter having designed the delightful Indian Garden Temple (Fig. 6). These early experiments in using Hindoo decoration soon had an important influence in the developing Regency style in England; the Royal Pavilion at Brighton being one of the more spectacular developments.

The Chinese style was in vogue in the 18th and early 19th centuries, when it was used in the garden for bridges, temples, dairies, and pagodas (Plate 7). Sir William Chambers had first created an interest in Chinese garden buildings when in 1757 he had published his book *Designs of Chinese Buildings* and in 1772 his *Dissertation on Oriental Gardening* and when in 1762 at the Royal Gardens at Kew he built his famous Pagoda (Fig. 2) and a bridge in a freely adapted but imaginative Chinese manner. As a young man William Chambers voyaged with the Swedish East India Company—he was born in Sweden— to Canton where he developed a taste for Chinese architecture and made many drawings of existing buildings. At Kew he was happy to use both the classical and the Chinese style for the design of his garden buildings. In the classical style he built a magnifi-

FIG. 6. Indian garden temple, Sezincote, Gloucestershire

cent orangery, the Temple of Bellona, and the Temple of Aeolus, which are still carefully maintained in what are now the Royal Botanic Gardens. Copies abroad of the English landscape park often have at least one Chinese garden building, and indeed the informal landscape style on the Continent became known as the 'Jardin Anglo-Chinois'.

The word pagoda is thought to have been brought to Europe by the Portuguese, who described any oriental temple as a pagoda. In 18th-century England it was used to describe a Buddhist temple which was built in the form of a tower.

The architect John Nash designed a fanciful pagoda for St. James's Park in the summer of 1814, as a part of the great Jubilee festival. The pagoda was seven storeys high and was erected by the side of a wooden bridge that spanned the ornamental water, and which was built to resemble the Rialto Bridge in Venice. Every part of the pagoda and the bridge was illuminated—partly by the newly introduced gas lamps—for the evening's festivities. Later in the evening the pagoda formed the main stage for the grand firework display. Catherine wheels and rockets burst out from every part of the building, which with the reflections in the water made a magnificent display. Unfortunately the firework display went farther than was planned when the pagoda itself caught fire and the five upper storeys fell crashing into the water. The bridge, however, remained intact until it was replaced in

[1] His mother was daughter of John Jackson, the nephew and heir of Samuel Pepys, the diarist.

1827, when the formal layout of the park was swept away and replaced by the present picturesque landscape.

The 'gentleman architect' Sanderson Miller was one of the earliest exponents of the Gothic style in garden buildings and picturesque ruins. Sanderson Miller was a Warwickshire squire who lived at Radway Grange, near Edgehill. At Radway, Miller made a large lawn with shady walks up to the top of the Edgehill escarpment where he built in 1750 a battlemented mock fortress and tower known now as Miller's Tower or Radway Tower (Fig. 7). It was built on the spot said to have been where King

FIG. 7.   Sanderson Miller's tower, Edgehill, Warwickshire

Charles I raised his standard at the Battle of Edgehill in October 1642. The Tower when completed was an admirable object to be seen from the grounds of Radway Grange, and it could also be used to entertain Miller's considerable circle of friends. For this latter purpose the Tower, which was octagonal, contained a similarly shaped room, with painted glass in the windows and alcoves for displaying statues. The Tower originally had a drawbridge leading to it from the gatehouse, but this has since disappeared. The present-day use of Miller's Tower is as a public house known as the Castle Inn.

Sanderson Miller had a hand in the design of many other well-known Gothic garden features, such as the Gothic arch that spans the drive at Lacock Abbey, Wiltshire, a Gothic ruin at Hagley, near Birmingham, in 1753, and a similar Gothic castle ruin for Lord Harwicke at Wimpole Hall, Cambridgeshire. The ruin at Wimpole Hall was built towards the end of the 1740's, and was sited so as to crown the hill at the end of one of the main

avenues.   In 1767, Capability Brown was commissioned to carry out improvements to the park at Wimpole, and was able to make a more appropriate landscape setting for Miller's uninhabitable but eye-catching ruined 'castle'. Horace Walpole (1717-1797), the champion of the picturesque landscape movement and the Gothic Revival, was greatly pleased with Miller's work, especially the ruin at Hagley of which he wrote that 'it would get him the freedom even of Strawberry,[1] it has the true rust of the Barons' Wars'.

William Shenstone (1714-1763), the poet and pioneer landscape theorist and practitioner at his own estate at the Leasowes, near Birmingham, gives perhaps the best account of the charms of ruins in the landscape in his essay *Unconnected Thoughts on Gardening:*

> Ruinated structures appear to derive their power of pleasing from the irregularity of surface, which is VARIETY; and the latitude they afford the imagination, to conceive an enlargement of their dimensions, or to recollect any events or circumstances appertaining to their pristine grandeur, so far as concerns grandeur and solemnity. The breaks in them should be as bold and abrupt as possible—If mere beauty be aimed at (which, however, is not their chief excellence) the waving line, with more easy transitions, will become of greater importance—Events relating to them may be simulated by numberless little artifices; but it is ever to be remembered, that high hills and sudden descents are most suitable to castles; and fertile vales, near wood and water, most imitative of the usual situations for abbeys and religious houses; large oaks, in particular, are essential to these latter.

The fashion for building ruins and follies to decorate the garden and park soon had an immense vogue throughout England. Some follies were designed by architects and landscape architects, but others were the owners' inventions, or were simply copies from other designs or actual ruins existing elsewhere. Many were rather flimsy structures built of plaster, timber and canvas, and soon disintegrated. A certain amount of decay, of course, was encouraged and this together with pine trees, ivy, owls and bats all greatly added to the enjoyment of the melancholy scene.

Follies include everything from eye-catchers and ruins to towers, mock castles, and sham bridges. William Kent in laying out the grounds at Rousham, Oxfordshire, had as early as 1738 built an eye-catcher in the form of a three-arched screen which when viewed from the terrace gave the impression of a ruined castle on the skyline. False bridges, that in fact were only painted

[1] Strawberry Hill, Twickenham, where Horace Walpole had altered an old house into the famous and fanciful Gothic castle. It is now a Roman Catholic training college.

timber screens, usually placed so as to make two lakes at different levels appear as one grand stretch of water, were also used by many 18th-century landscape designers. The well-known sham bridge at Kenwood, by Hampstead Heath, London, is a good example of the period. However, the greater proportion of follies were built by eccentric amateur architects, who had at some time an irresistible desire to erect these strange but original buildings in the grounds of their park or on some near-by promontory. Their heyday coincided with the picturesque style in landscape gardening, that is from the early 18th century until the middle of the 19th century.

Critics, who are also purists so far as Gothic architecture is concerned, have since deplored these follies and in particular their misuse of Gothic form, structure, and material. Their influence on the more serious art of architecture was, of course, deplorable, and helped to produce a few decades later many grotesque Victorian edifices. But as garden decoration they were imaginative, full of fun and fantasy, and refreshingly free from academic rules.

The West Country seems to have been particularly well supplied with folly builders. Lord Bathhurst with the aid of the poet Alexander Pope built in the woods of his park at Cirencester,

FIG. 8.   Sham castle, Cirencester Park, Gloucestershire

Gloucestershire, in 1721, a sham castle (Fig. 8) which was supposed to have been mistaken by one antiquarian of the time as one of King Arthur's castles. This mock castle still exists and is now known as King Arthur's Folly. A mock castle was also built in the park at Badminton, Gloucestershire, in about 1750, and still exists. Another West Country folly builder was the Messiter family, who in order to provide work during a severe depression in the glove-making industry in Yeovil had four follies and a grotto built in the park at Barwick, Somerset. The follies are at the four main points of the compass from the house, and at the

boundary of the park. The one known as 'Jack the Treacle Eater' is a particularly delightful folly. The statue of Hermes crowns the tower which is supported by an arch. The local legend has it that Hermes represents a local man named Jack who, because he was such a good long-distance runner, took messages for the Messiter family to as far afield as London, and whose training diet was mostly composed of treacle

Prospect towers were popular subjects for amateur architects about this time (Fig. 9). The tower if sited on high ground would provide a splendid panoramic view, and act as a landmark and perhaps recall romantic associations with a particular hill.

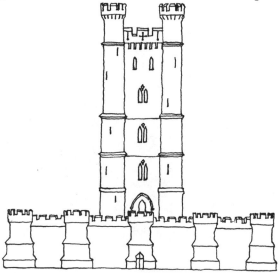

FIG. 9.   Prospect tower, Alton Towers, Staffordshire, from
J. C. Loudon's *An Encyclopaedia of Gardening*, 1834

Sanderson Miller's Tower at Edgehill, as already mentioned, was supposedly the spot where King Charles raised his standard before the Battle of Edgehill; and Alfred's Tower, a brick triangular structure at Kingsettle Hill, three miles from Stourhead, Wiltshire, was erected in 1772 on the spot where King Alfred is said to have set up his standard against the Danes in A.D. 879. Prospect towers continued to be built in parks throughout the 19th century. At Rous Lench, Worcestershire, a very fine look-out tower was built on high ground at the end of the garden in the 19th century. It is built in red brick and has a machicolated top resembling an Italian campanile (Fig. 10). Often the prospect tower was called a belvedere (from the Italian *bel vedere*—a fine view) and were then designed in the Italian style. In Renaissance Italy the belvedere was a tower or turret mostly built on to a building so as to afford a view over the city wall to the surrounding countryside.

The last great folly building took place in the gardens at Alton Towers, Staffordshire, in the first half of the 19th century. The follies included a prospect tower (Fig. 9) (but it was not built on the highest part of the estate), a Druid's Sideboard and an imitation Stonehenge.

After about 1840 folly building largely ceased, so far as the park and garden were concerned; instead garden ornament was concerned with the more practical matters of horticulture and scientific instruction. Eccentricity moved away from the garden to the design of the house itself and produced such wonders as the Royal Pavilion at Brighton; Fonthill Abbey, Wiltshire; Hadlow Castle, Kent (Fig. 11); and Alfred Waterhouse's rebuilding of Eaton Hall. By the time Sir Joseph Paxton was planning the grounds for the permanent home for the Crystal Palace at Sydenham in South London, a folly in the garden would have been unthinkable, unless you include carpet bedding as a folly, in

7.   Chinese pagoda, Woburn Abbey, Bedfordshire

which case it was unintentional! The large concrete monsters in the park at Sydenham may look like follies now, but to the serious-minded Victorian they were there for the purpose of instructing the populace in palæontology, zoology and geology,

FIG. 10.   Look-out tower, Rous Lench, Worcestershire

the latter science dictating of course the arrangement of rocks into the correct geological strata and sequence!

The popularity of grottoes outlasted the craze for folly building, for the Victorians adopted the 18th-century grotto as a means of decorating parts of the conservatory (Plate 8). Grottoes had, of course, been built in some of the Renaissance villa gardens in Italy, where they were decorated with fossilised figures, bones, spars, stalactites and running water to excite sublime if not horrific emotions. In Britain the shell room was to some extent the forerunner of the grotto, certainly so far as much of its decoration is concerned. The beautiful shell room at Woburn Abbey, Bedfordshire, which has been recently cleaned and now has its original clear colours and sparkle, dates from the middle of the 17th century. The shell house at Goodwood, Sussex, built in 1739, was designed as a pavilion but decorated inside with most beautiful shellwork. Sarah, the second Duchess of Richmond, with some help from her family, spent seven years making the shell decoration at Goodwood. These shell houses showed the attractive effects that could be obtained from the painstaking use of shells as decoration, for the finished effect was a cheerful one and did not attempt to convey any of the gloom and melancholy so sought after by the later grotto builders.

Alexander Pope (1688-1744) can be said to have really started the fashion for building grottoes in Britain when he constructed in 1720 his famous grot in his garden at Twickenham, Middlesex.

Pope's garden at Twickenham was on both sides of a highway with the more extensive part on the higher side away from the river Thames. In order to overcome this obstacle he constructed a passage under the road. He then transformed the passage into a grotto, with the main entrance opposite the river and formed of rough stonework. The grotto and the garden which contained a shell temple, an orangery, and an obelisk, occupied Pope's interest for much of his life, and was visited by the fashionable and literary world. Pope's own delightful description of the grotto is as follows:

I have just put the last hand to my works of this kind, in happily finishing the subterraneous way and grotto. I found there a spring of the clearest water, which falls in a perpetual rill, that echoes through the cavern night and day. From the river Thames you see through an ivy arch, up a walk of the wilderness, to a kind of open temple wholly composed of shells in the rustic manner; and from that distance, under the temple, you look down through a sloping arcade of trees, and see the sails on the river passing suddenly and vanishing, as through a perspective glass. When you shut the door of this grotto, it becomes on the instant, from a luminous room, a camera obscura, on the walls of which all the objects of the river, hills, woods, and boats, are forming a moving picture, in their visible radiations; and when you have a mind to light it less, it affords you a very different scene. It is finished with shells, interspersed with looking-glass in regular forms, and in the ceiling is a

FIG. 11.   Hadlow Castle, Kent.   (House now demolished)

star of the same material, at which when a lamp of an orbicular figure of thin alabaster is hung in the middle, a thousand pointed rays glitter, and are reflected over the place. There are connected to this grotto, by a narrow passage, two porches; one towards the river, of smooth stones, full of light and open; the other towards the garden, shadowed with trees, rough with shells, flints, and iron ore. The bottom is paved with simple pebbles, as is also the adjoining walk up the wilderness to the temple, in the natural taste, agreeing not ill with the little dripping murmur, and the aquatic idea of the whole place. It wants nothing to complete it but a good statue with an inscription, like that beautiful antique one which you know of.[1] You will think I have been very poetical in this description; but it is pretty near the truth.

[1] Pope's translation of this is carved in stone beside the Nymph of the Grot at Stourhead.

Doctor Johnson, as could be expected, saw little that was amusing or entertaining in Pope's passion for landscape gardening and grotto making, and after the poet's death wrote:

A grotto is not often the wish or pleasure of an Englishman, who has more frequent need to solicit than to exclude the sun; but Pope's excavation was requisite as an entrance to his garden, and, as some men try to be proud of their defects, he extracted an ornament from an inconvenience, and variety produced a grotto where necessity enforced a passage.

The grotto at Twickenham still survives, and is listed as a Grade I building of architectural and historic interest by the local planning authority.

Most of the best grottoes that followed Pope's example were

8. Grotto in the conservatory, Rousham, Oxfordshire

constructed as tunnels into hillsides or under or near to ponds and lakes. They often took many years to complete and their decoration would consist of elaborate designs in shells, scallops, spars, marbles, broken glass, bones, crystals, stalactites, cobbles, and sculptured lions, serpents, neptunes, and nymphs. Sometimes the grotto would have several rooms or chambers reached by a tunnel. The rooms might have a cold bath, or be used for gambling or other suitable gatherings, or simply be domed to give a terrifying echo.

One of the most celebrated grottoes was at Oatlands Park, Surrey, which regrettably was demolished in 1948. It was said to have taken five years to build and to have cost several thousands of pounds. It had three rooms, a tuffa entrance and a view to the lake, a cascade, a gaming room and a cold bath with a statue of the Medici Venus placed as if ready to take a plunge. The upper chamber received daylight from skylights and was the favourite room of the Duchess of York, who took many of her meals there. It is thought that the Oatlands grotto, like the earlier but smaller grotto at Pains Hill, Surrey, was built by Josiah Lane and his son of Tisbury or Westbury, who became an authority on the building of grottoes and rockwork. Josiah Lane was also employed by Lord Arundel to build a grotto at Wardour Castle, in 1792. This grotto is built in stone, brick, and tuffa, and decorated with ammonites, mosses, and ferns, and with holes for framing views of the park.

The grotto at Stourhead, Wiltshire, whilst not so highly decorated or as extensive as many of the more celebrated ones of the 18th century, is nevertheless a very striking and well constructed grot, and one that is in a good state of preservation. Stourhead is now National Trust property, and the grotto is open to the public. The main chamber of the grotto is vaulted and has bench seats from whence a fine view is afforded across the lake, almost at eye-level, as the floor is below that of the water-level of the lake. This main chamber contains a bath which is also one of the sources of the river Stour. At the back of the bath is an alcove containing a reclining statue in whitened lead of the Nymph of the Grot by the sculptor Rysbrack. The Nymph is dramatically lit by a shaft of daylight coming from an opening in the roof of the grotto. At the side of the bath are carved some lines, translated by Alexander Pope during a stay at Stourhead, of a Latin inscription by Cardinal Bembo:

> Nymph of the Grot these sacred springs I keep
> And to the murmur of these waters sleep
> Ah! spare my slumbers, gentle tread the cave,
> And drink in silence or in silence lave.

Farther along from the Nymph is another alcove where a statue of Neptune by Rysbrack is again dramatically illuminated by a piercing shaft of daylight. Stourhead contains many other

FIG. 12.   The Pantheon, Stourhead, Wiltshire

typical and beautiful garden buildings from the 18th century, including a miniature replica of the Pantheon (Fig. 12), a Temple of the Sun, a prospect tower (Alfred's Tower), a rustic cottage, a well-head and two tuffa arches (Fig. 13).

Tuffa with its holes, spikes and aqueous shapes was a favourite material for garden archways and grottoes and for constructing the typical conservatory grotto in the 19th century (Plate 8). Tuffa stone was obtained from the West Country, principally from around Bath, in limestone country, where the springs have water that is charged with soluble calcium bicarbonate which, on reaching the surface, leaves an insoluble carbonate known as tuffa on the surrounding limestone rock.

The 18th-century landowner with his taste for picturesque scenery did not always rest contented with follies and grottoes, or

Seventeenth century gazebo, Packwood House, Warwickshire

Eighteenth century pavilion, Farnborough Hall, Warwickshire

Robert Adam's bridge, Compton Verney, Warwickshire

Furness Railway seat in author's garden

Corkscrew fountain, Alton Towers, Staffordshire

Sundial in the garden of Penfound Manor, Cornwall

Sculpture by Jack Dawson, Corley Residential School,
near Coventry

Garden of Contemplation, Cannon Hill Park, Birmingham
Parks Department

Play sculpture by John Bridgeman, Curtis Gardens, Birmingham
Parks Department

Topiary garden, Compton Wynyates, Warwickshire

Alton Towers, Staffordshire

Pleached hornbeam garden, Hidcote Manor, Gloucestershire

Italian well-head, Penfound Manor, Cornwall

Fountains in the lake, Jephson Gardens, Leamington Spa

Florentine wrought iron gates, Penfound Manor, Cornwall

Chinese Pagoda, Alton Towers, Staffordshire

the association of objects, for exciting his sense of the melancholy and the sublime. Text-books of the day, such as William Wrighte's *Gothic Architecture or Rural Amusement* published in 1767, included not only drawings of Chinese, Gothic, or natural grottoes, baths, mosques, grotesque and rustic seats, but also for huts, retreats, and summer and winter hermitages. What could be more interesting and cosy than to have a recluse leading the life of a hermit in a rustic hut in the park, and to see on a calm winter's day the hermit's chimney smoke rising from some distant part of the landscape? Certainly it could be an amusing novelty to point out to guests. If the hermit's hut or cave could be sited in a wild part of the park, with rocks and pine trees, why the scene would look like a painting by Salvator Rosa, whose paintings of wild romantic scenery were beginning to be as keenly sought after as

FIG. 13. Tuffa arch, Stourhead, Wiltshire

the more peaceful and pastoral scenes depicted by Claude Lorraine.

The hermit's house was above all else rustic, both in appearance and construction, and few have survived to the present day. Some were more accurately known as root-houses, as they were built principally of tree roots, bark, ivy branches, and thatch, and so had an even more weird and grotesque appearance. Whilst their construction was easily managed by estate craftsmen, the hermits themselves were a more difficult problem. There were many advertisements for hermits, who were usually expected to sign an agreement whereby for certain payments they were to live strictly the life of a recluse in the park. No doubt the agreement became more specific as experience was gained of the frailties of some of the paid hermits, who had to be dismissed for consorting with female servants, or visiting the local inn!

A number of writers were quick to parody the fanciful whims of some estate owners in their search for novelty in park and garden ornament. Robert Morris in his book *Architecture Improved* published in 1755 inserted the following advertisement:

'There is now in the Press . . . A Treatise on Country Five Barr'd Gates, Stiles and Wickets, elegant Pig-styes, beautiful Henhouses, and delightful Cow-cribs, superb Cart-houses, magnificent Barn Doors, variegated Barn Racks, and admirable Sheep-Folds; according to the Turkish and Persian manner. . . . To which is added, some Designs of Fly-traps, Bee Palaces and Emmet Houses, in the Muscovite and Arabian architecture; all adapted to the Latitude and Genius of England. The whole entirely new, and inimitably designed in Two Parts, on Forty Pewter Plates, under the immediate inspection of Don Gulielmus De Demi Je ne sai Quoi, chief Architect to the Grand Signor.'

Contorted branches, roots, ivy branches, bark and thatch were of course readily available in rural areas, and fairly easily put together to form many other rustic adornments besides homes for hermits. All manner of rustic arches, pergolas, seats, shelters, summer-houses, and aviaries became popular ornaments for the Victorian garden, most of them being crude and unattractive. The fashion reached its height after Shirley Hibberd, an influential writer on gardening and garden design in the middle of the 19th century, wrote *Rustic Adornments for Homes of Taste* which was published in 1856. However, the Victorian garden, as already mentioned, had usually to be arranged on scientific and utilitarian lines; the sense of frivolity and fun which had gone to the lengths of producing hermits' houses in the 18th century was to have little influence in the 19th. Garden buildings must now have a utilitarian purpose. 'Nothing gives more general satisfaction than a neat and comfortable picturesque cottage, with a good garden, in neat order and cultivation; and such buildings may always be applied to some useful purpose, even in the grounds of small villas or *fermes ornées*. In more extensive scenes,' continued J. C. Loudon,[1] 'cottages of different styles may be introduced, from that of the Greenlander or Norwegian to the Hindoo; and there can be no reason why a proprietor, if he chooses to go to the expense, and will attend to the comfort of the interior, should not ornament the dwelling of an upper servant in any Style he pleases, even that of a Chinese mandarin.'

The most universal garden building since the Regency period has been the summer-house. At first these summer-houses were built in a rustic manner, often circular in plan, with walls of contorted branches and bark, with windows sometimes glazed

[1] *An Encyclopaedia of Gardening*, 1834.

9.   Early 19th-century summer-house, Charlecote, Warwickshire

with coloured glass, and a thatched roof (Plate 9), but other more exotic styles, such as Byzantium, were used (Fig. 14).

Shirley Hibberd in the *National Magazine* of 1857 gave a very thorough description for the design of a rustic summer-house. Hibberd recommended that the main construction should be formed from unbarked timber, and selected toppings of old apple trees for the lattice work. The apple branches should be varnished, 'so as to stand out brightly amongst the darker portions of unbarked timber'. Oak was thought to be best for the unbarked main timbers. For the treatment of the rustic apple branches Hibberd advised that 'they should be sawed up into proper lengths, and then steeped in boiling water to loosen the bark; then

FIG. 14. Summer-house in the Byzantium style, from *The National Magazine*, 1857

well dried, worked into their places, and varnished. Against the more massive portions of the building they contrast very prettily.' To varnish rustic woodwork he recommended the following procedure:

'Wash the woodwork with soap and water; and when dry, wash it again with boiled linseed oil, choosing a hot sunny day for the operation. A few days after, varnish it twice with hard varnish, and it will last for years. To give a dark oak colour to

rough wood, another plan may be adopted. Take a quart of linseed-oil and two ounces of asphaltum, and boil over a slow fire till the asphaltum is dissolved, stirring the while. This is not sticky, and lasts for years. As the ingredients are terribly inflammable, the boiling had to be done out of doors'.

Hibberd thought that bark or thatch were the best materials for the roof. For a really first-class summer-house a camera-obscura could be fitted into the dome which would 'increase the attractions of the retreat'.

The rustic summer-house is best sited on a mound surrounded by shrubs and trees, rootwork, rockeries, ferneries and water scenery; never should it 'be placed in clean open spots of grass and flowers'.

Mosshouses—a type of rustic summer-house—were popular garden buildings in the Victorian garden. Many lady gardeners spent as much time designing mosshouses as their grandmothers had in making shell-houses and shell-decorated grottoes. Mrs. Loudon wrote that 'some of the handsomest mosshouses in England have been erected in Bagshot Park, the seat of the Duchess of Gloucester, by her Royal Highness's very intelligent gardener, Mr. Toward'. Mosshouses were made from a framework of young larch or pine trees to which a lattice of laths was added. Between the laths a number of different mosses were pushed until the whole rustic arbour was covered over. Sometimes the moss was further fixed by wire, cord, and nails. 'The great art', wrote Mrs. Loudon, 'consists in arranging the moss so as to form a pattern: and this is accomplished by sorting the moss into heaps of the different colours, tracing the pattern rudely on the laths, and keeping a coloured copy.' Many different species of mosses and lichens were collected for the covering of the mosshouse. Mrs. Loudon recommended four different species of terrestrial mosses, as well as the reindeer lichen which could be collected from the branches of ash trees, or from heathlands. The roof was normally thatched, but was occasionally covered with moss-covered bark from old oak or pine trees.

Root houses were another type of rustic summer-house that was often built in Victorian gardens. They were built from roots of trees, including the stool or base of tree trunks, and were usually roofed in heath thatch. Roots were also used in association with plants and stones to form a contrast with the 'smoothness and high art displayed on the general surface of the lawn'.

An ice-house was an indispensable amenity for a large country house in Britain during the 18th century and throughout much of the 19th century. The ice-house could store ice for two or three

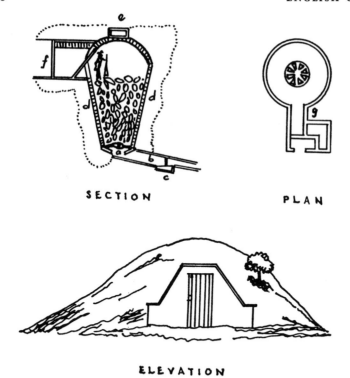

SECTION   PLAN

ELEVATION

FIG. 15.   Construction of an ice-house, from J. C. Loudon's
An Encyclopaedia of Gardening, 1834

years by taking in ice during the winter and keeping it dry and cool throughout the summer.   To achieve this the ice-house had to be sited near a pond or lake which was sometimes specially dug for the purpose.   The land on which the ice-house was built had to be well drained either naturally if on sandy soil or by raising the ice-well above the ground level and constructing a system of land drainage.

The shape of many ice-houses is circular in plan, with a conical roof, and these are nearly always attractive in appearance. occasionally an ice-house was made to resemble a classical temple in the park or garden.   The building would if possible be sited on the northern slope of a hillside and trees were planted to give further shade and coolness.   The ice-well had to be dry, and so was often sunk into an artificial raised mound.   J. C. Loudon's *An Encyclopaedia of Gardening*, published in 1834, has a sectional drawing (Fig. 15) showing the construction of a typical ice-house of the 19th century.   In this drawing (*a*) represents a grate to let

moisture drain away from the ice-well; (*b*) drain; (*c*) trap to exclude air; (*d*) sides of wall made from brick or stonework, 2 feet deep; (*e*) hole for putting in new ice; (*f*) door for taking out ice; (*g*) porch, filled with straw and three doors.   In Loudon's design the whole building was covered with soil.   The ice had to be packed and well rammed into the ice-well, so as to exclude air, and if snow instead of ice was used, then this had to be packed until it excluded all air and resembled ice.

The upper chamber of some ice-houses contained a cold storage room.   By the 1870's ice-making machines were taking the place of ice-houses, although they continued to be used by some country houses up until the 20th century.   Some of the conical-shaped ice-houses display fine craftsmanship in stone or brickwork and are worthy of preservation from an architectural standpoint, and a few others because of their siting are an attractive addition to the landscape park.   At Linley Hall, Shropshire, the ice-house has been built to resemble a classical temple.   It is sited on a promontory by the lake where it makes a fine eye-catching feature in the park landscape.

The summer-house could be used for tea parties, especially for the children; for private study or contemplation; or for simply storing garden furniture and equipment for the new craze for games in the garden, such as croquet, lawn tennis, clock golf and badminton.   This latter use, more often than not, dictated the siting of Victorian and Edwardian summer-houses, for they were mostly built adjoining the lawn that had been levelled for croquet or lawn tennis, and shaded by such favourite evergreen trees as the cedar of Lebanon or the ilex.

By the 20th century summer-houses were beginning to be designed on more straightforward carpentry lines, devoid of fuss and ornamentation, but possessing little elegance and delight—qualities that a garden building should surely always possess. Since the First World War the desire to get sun-tanned each year —which is now so firmly associated with health and beauty—has naturally influenced the garden house.   More leisure and less working in the open-air will no doubt help to keep the sun-bathing cult with us for many years to come.   The garden building of today is most likely to be a summer-house, or a children's playhouse built to receive as much of the sun as possible, or even, as was the vogue in the 1920's and '30's, built on a revolving platform so that it could be turned to face the sun at all times of the day.

Chapter Two

GARDEN FURNITURE

Mediaeval turf seats; 18th-century timber seats in the classical, Chinese and Gothic styles; siting of seats; roofed seats; movable seats; wrought and cast iron seats; public house tables; wirework furniture; cast iron boot scrapers, garden notices and mushroom seats; painting of garden furniture; stone and marble seats; steamer and deck chairs; straw and wickerwork furniture; some contemporary examples.

AS the art and science of garden making has advanced, the garden has become more furnished with objects which help to make for the ideal environment. The mediaeval gardens provided food, medicinal herbs, flowers, fountains and well-heads for the domestic water supply, sundials for recording time, space for outdoor games, as well as a place for visual pleasure and relaxation. In more recent times the garden has also provided an opportunity for the enjoyment of such elemental pleasures as sunbathing, paddling and swimming, or simply eating and generally relaxing in the open air. The most successful garden design is based on the requirements of the user, whether it is a family, a group of school children or a local community. Thinking of the garden as being something more than a picture to be looked at from the house, but rather as a pleasant setting for a variety of human activities, has meant that the garden has had to have its own special furnishings. Much of this furniture has been very decorative and can be rightly considered as garden ornament.

The most elementary piece of furniture is something for sitting on. The earliest garden seats were made of turf; there are many references to them in mediaeval writings and they are shown in several mediaeval illustrations. They were made by building up soil to the required height and retaining it with a wattle hurdle or a brick wall. Turf was then grown on the top to form the seat. The turf would usually be planted with low-growing wild flowers. William Lawson as late as 1618 in his book *A New Orchard and Garden* recommended that for banks and seats 'camamile, penny-royal, daisies and violets are seemly and comfortable'. The turf seat must have had much simple rustic charm, but was hardly suited to our damp climate, and with the influence of the Renaissance arts on garden design in this country the construction of outdoor seats became the province of the carpenter, joiner and stonemason.

The most popular material for garden seats in the Renaissance garden in England in the 17th century was timber. After the Restoration, taste became more extravagant, and wealthy owners of large houses wished to furnish them in the style of the great Renaissance palaces on the Continent. The local craftsmen whose methods and designs were handed down from craftsman to pupil, had not the knowledge or taste to provide these new styles from the Continent. Consequently, architects and designers who had perhaps travelled and studied abroad, or at least were well versed in the new fashions, not only designed furnishings for their new buildings but soon found a ready demand for their pattern books. In the first half of the 18th century there was a constant stream of publications giving designs and patterns for furniture. These books were used by craftsmen throughout the country to meet the demand for more variety and elegance in domestic furniture. Whilst most of these books were concerned with furniture for the house, a number of authors, mostly architects, produced designs for garden furniture that could be made in timber. Some of these seats have survived, but the engravings from the many pattern books give the fullest picture of the garden furniture of this period. To begin with, the designs and the style of decoration were inspired from ancient Greece and Rome, and this remained the main influence throughout the 18th century. But there were other influences, in particular those from the romantic Far East, and from mediaeval art in the form of Gothic, or as it was sometimes called, Saxon decoration.

William Kent (1685-1748), who began his career as a painter, but who became a much more successful and gifted architect, and according to Horace Walpole, 'the father of modern landscape gardening', also liked to design the furniture for the large country houses which he was commissioned to build. His style for furniture was designed to be in keeping with his Palladian architecture. Most of the motifs for Kent's furniture came from ancient Rome. He was a brilliant designer, and surviving pieces of furniture have a boldness and a directness that is immediately pleasing. The furniture that he designed for the garden was mostly for the temples or arcades that had a good view and therefore demanded some form of seating. Kent's landscape designs, although few in number, had a great influence and helped to improve the general standard of taste in the country at that time.

Batty Langley (1696-1751), and his brother Thomas (b. 1702), through their many publications of designs for garden buildings and furniture, also had a considerable influence on garden ornament at this time. Batty Langley was an architect, furniture designer, and landscape gardener, and his brother was an engraver and draughtsman. They are perhaps best remembered for their designs for garden buildings and furniture in the Gothic and grotesque manner. These designs very much helped to create the

vogue for the grotesque and the rustic in certain parts of the garden in the 18th century. A typical rustic chair thought to be most appropriate for a hermit's cell or for a Gothic summer-house is shown in Fig. 16. It is one of the designs from Robert Manwaring's book *The Cabinet and Chair-Maker's Real Friend and Companion, or, the whole system of chair-making made plain and easy; containing upwards of one hundred new and useful designs for all sorts of chairs* . . . published in 1765. These rustic chairs were

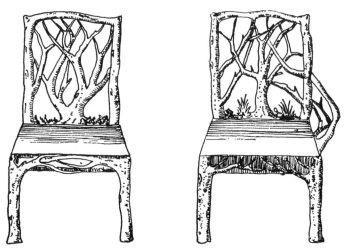

FIG. 16. Rustic chairs for a hermit's cell, or a Gothic summer-house, from Robert Manwaring's *The Cabinet and Chair-Maker's Real Friend and Companion* . . . 1765

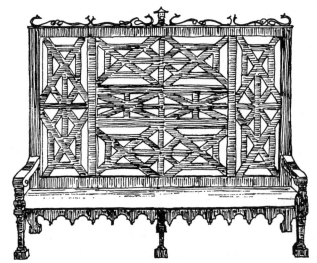

FIG. 17. Design for a Chinese garden seat from William Halfpenny's *New Designs for Chinese Temples*, 1750

10. Wrought iron garden chair,
Hidcote Manor, Gloucestershire

11. Wrought iron garden chairs,
Lanhydrock House, Cornwall

'supposed to be executed with the limbs of yew, apple, or pear trees, ornamented with leaves and blossoms, which if properly painted will appear like Nature'.

The Chinese taste in decoration was also considered as being particularly appropriate for garden furniture, and was an influence that lasted in the garden throughout the 18th century and during the Regency period. One of the earliest exponents of the Chinese style was the architect and carpenter, William Halfpenny (d. 1755). Fig. 17 shows a design for a garden seat in the Chinese taste from Halfpenny's book *New Designs for Chinese Temples*, published in 1750. Sir William Chambers, an architect who built a number of Chinese garden buildings, including the famous Pagoda at Kew, had actually travelled to China where he made his own first-hand sketches of Chinese buildings and ornament. Chambers, like Kent, was a leading architect of the day and a most gifted designer. Many of his designs for garden furniture appeared in his book *Designs of Chinese Buildings, Furniture, Dresses, Machines and Utensils . . . From the originals drawn in China by Mr. Chambers, Architect*, published in 1757. But Halfpenny and Chambers were not the only designers advocating the oriental style. Charles Over, for example, was the author of *Ornamental Architecture in the Gothic, Chinese and Modern Taste*, published in 1758, which contained over fifty designs 'many of which may be executed with roots of trees for gardens, parks, forests, woods, canals, etc.' Fig. 18 is from Over's book and shows a garden seat in the 'Chinese Taste of Small Expense, genteel and durable'. The spate of books giving designs for garden ornament and furniture that were published in the 18th century meant that there was a steady demand for the instruction they offered.

Within a very short space of time the design of garden seats progressed from the most rudimentary of conceptions—the mediaeval turf seat—to the well-made and beautifully proportioned seats constructed from the drawings of the leading architects of the day. The inspiration for the decoration and style came from the ornament of ancient Rome, the Orient, Gothic art, or simple rusticity. Often the designs were a mixture of styles, especially those claiming to be Chinese, which were more likely to be seats in the Classical mould with applied Chinese motifs.

The style of a garden seat was chosen according to its position in the garden. This was a most significant development in the appreciation of scenery, for no longer was the aim in garden making to make each and every landscape the same, that is as formal and as obviously man-made as possible. The emphasis in the 18th century was on the elements of variety, surprise and

FIG. 18.   Design for a Chinese garden seat from Charles Over's *Ornamental Architecture in the Gothic, Chinese, and Modern Taste*, 1758

concealment, and these were to be obtained from natural scenery. The new attitude to garden design was described by many writers and poets in the 18th century. The noblest expression of this approach was written by Alexander Pope in his 'Essay on Man'.

To build, to plant, whatever you intend,
To rear the Column, or the arch to bend,
To swell the Terras, or sink the Grot;
In all let Nature never be forgot.
But treat the Goddess like a modest fair,
Nor over-dress, nor leave her wholly bare;
Let not each beauty ev'ry where be spy'd,
Where half the skill is decently to hide.
He gains all points, who pleasingly confounds,
Surprizes, varies, and conceals the Bounds.
Consult the Genius of the place in all;
That tells the Waters or to rise, or fall;
Or helps th'ambitious Hill the Heav'ns to scale,
Or scoops in circling theatres the Vale;
Calls in the country, catches op'ning glades,
Joins willing woods, and varies shades from shades;
Now breaks, or now directs, th'intending Lines;
Paints as you plant, and, as you work, designs.
 Still follow sense, of ev'ry Art the Soul,
Parts answering parts shall slide into a whole,
Spontaneous beauties all around advance,
Start ev'n from Difficulty, strike from Chance;
Nature shall join you; Time shall make it grow
A Work to wonder at—perhaps a STOW.'

This change in attitude affected in no small way the furniture of the picturesque landscape garden. Rustic or Gothic seats would be used in the wilder or more rugged scenery in the garden, whilst the Classical or Chinese-styled seats would be sited in the softer landscape of gently curving topography and prospect. Chinese buildings would greatly 'diversify a scene' and bring an exotic touch to a corner of the landscape garden, and it was essential that these buildings should be fully furnished in the Chinese taste. One of the earliest landscape gardens laid out on the principle of 'consulting the genius of the place' was the Leasowes, at Halesowen, near Birmingham. It was laid out by its owner William Shenstone early in the 18th century. Shenstone's garden together with his writings on landscape design are today better remembered than his poetry. J. Dodsley's two volumes of Shenstone's works in verse and prose, give a plan and a description of the garden at the Leasowes, which is a most valuable record of this once-famous garden that has now largely disappeared in the urban growth of the Midlands. Dodsley's description takes the reader on the designed route around the landscaped grounds, which contained many carefully sited seats 'chiefly intended as hints to spectators' to stop and admire the view. Most of these seats were timber benches, but there were also more elaborate structures such as a pyramidal seat, an octagon seat and a Gothic seat, as well as assignation seats suitably placed in Lovers' Walk.

The grounds to the larger and more magnificent country houses were usually in two parts; the landscape garden about the house, and the surrounding parkland—at Blenheim known as the Great Park. The two parts, of course, merged imperceptibly one into the other, the important difference being that the landscape about the house was designed to be seen on foot, whilst the Great Park would have its ride and was designed to be seen from a horse-drawn carriage. Seats were therefore mostly restricted to the landscape garden about the house, and were a most essential part of the planned route that every visitor would take through the gardens. A guide-book to Blenheim, published in 1814, for instance, refers to seats in the landscape garden, but not in the Great Park. They were sited in much the same way as Shenstone had pioneered at the Leasowes, as can be judged from the following description from the guide-book:

The occasional recurrence also of the garden chair, the plain bench, or the circular seat round the trunk of some umbrageous tree, by presenting opportunities for rest, prevent the idea of lassitude. Thus, in our journey through life, it is not always the actual use of the accommodations we possesss, that adds to our comfort; it is the reflection that we may command them in the hour of need, and that

we have it in our power to gratify the wish as soon as it is felt. But these are not simply objects of ornament and convenience; they generally point out scenes, which repose may contemplate with delight, and fancy combine into picture.

Much thought continued to be given to the choice of seats for a particular situation. As the garden became more varied and contained many more specialised parts, the successful selection became more difficult. Of all the many text-books on gardening in the 19th century, Mrs. Loudon's writings, addressed primarily to ladies, gave perhaps the best advice on the placing of seats in the garden. In her book *The Ladies' Companion to the Flower Garden*, she recommended that rustic seats should be confined to rustic parts of the garden, and that 'seats for a lawn or highly kept pleasure ground ought to be of comparatively simple and architectural forms, and either of wood or stone. . . .' Mrs. Loudon thought that notice should be taken of aspect, so that

FIG. 19. Pope's seat, Cirencester Park, Gloucestershire

some seats would be placed to receive the maximum amount of sunshine, whilst others should be in shade for use in hot weather. She rightly advised that garden seats look inviting and more indigenous to a scene if the backs are hidden by shrubs or trees. Finally she warned that seats should be so sited as to avoid 'any temptation to the person sitting on them to strain their eyes to the right or left, nor where the boundary of the garden forms a conspicuous object on the view'.

To afford some protection against the weather, which before the 20th century included strong sunshine as much as wind and rain, the seat was given a roof. The earliest form of seat protection was the arbour which was made of timber or iron lattice

12.   Wrought iron seat, Packwood House, Warwickshire

work and partly covered with climbing plants.   By the 18th century, roofed seats were usually more architectural in form and were built of stone; a typical example is Pope's seat at Cirencester Park, Gloucestershire (Fig. 19) which was erected at a spot especially liked by the poet.   Other architectural types of roofed seats took the form of porticoes and temples and, for wilder scenery, rustic structures such as moss houses, root huts and grottoes were erected.   In the 19th century the circular or octagonal summer-house built of timber with an overhanging thatch roof was a favourite form of protection for a fixed garden seat. These structures were normally open to the south so that they could be warmed by the low winter sun, but in summer, when the sun was higher, they would afford welcome shade.

Designers during the Regency period invented a number of very elegant structures made from iron, copper, and canvas for

FIG. 20.   Design for a covered garden seat from J. B. Papworth's
Rural Residences, 1818

covering garden seats. The architect J. B. Papworth at about this time was particularly imaginative in his designs for garden ornaments and for roofed seats. The roofing was either carried out in sheet metal such as copper (Fig. 20) or of canvas supported on an iron skeleton. These tent-like roofs in metal for garden seats and 'chiosks' were soon adopted as applied ornament for the house as roofs for balconies, verandahs, and porches, and became one of the chief characteristics of Regency architecture. Tent-like roofs continued to be used as canopies over garden seats throughout the 19th century. A quite ordinary slatted bench seat with cast iron ends in the rustic style could have a canvas canopy (Fig. 21) which could be rolled-up or let down again by

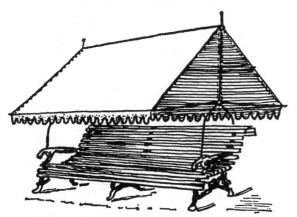

FIG. 21. Seat fitted with a movable canopy, from William Robinson's *The Parks, Promenades and Gardens of Paris*, 1869

means of a chain. These canopies were intended only as a shade against the sun, which may seem a little unusual today with our passion for getting sun-tanned or sun-burned! Advertisements for skin ointments in the 19th century would, for instance, make a point of claiming that the preparation would remove sunburn and tan.

In the last century there were a number of movable seats brought out for the garden. The most popular type was the wheelbarrow seat which, as the name implies, had one or sometimes two wheels at one end and two handles at the other which enabled it to be easily moved to different parts of the garden. These seats could also have the additional feature of a hinged back, which when not in use could be folded down over the seat so as to keep it dry and free from fouling by birds. The hinged back device was used on other types of garden seats, and although it was a good practical idea it unfortunately made the seat look

most forlorn when it was folded up. The wheelbarrow seat continued to be made into the early part of the 20th century, and was popular in Edwardian gardens. For fairly light garden seats castors were sometimes fitted to enable them to be moved about the garden (Fig. 34).

The really ubiquitous material in industrial Britain during the 19th century was iron, whether wrought or, as was more often the case, cast. Decorative wrought iron is slowly and expertly shaped into the desired forms by a craftsman. Each article in this material is therefore hand made. The process of its manufacture has been reflected in the restrained but elegant garden seats made in wrought iron in the 18th and 19th centuries. It is very noticeable how often the designs of these seats and chairs appear to have been inspired from 18th-century house furniture (Fig. 22). A number of wrought iron seats have backs and seats made up from small flat iron chains which are flexible enough to give a

FIG. 22. Wrought iron seat, Hidcote Manor, Gloucestershire

surprisingly comfortable seating (Plates 10 and 11). Most of these 19th-century wrought iron seats and chairs, because of their attractive appearance and genuine craftsmanship, are some of the most sought after garden ornaments (Plates 12 and 13). A word of warning must be given here against mistaking for wrought ironwork the poor imitations carried out in mild steel. These are inferior in every way as they are a misuse of mild steel, possess very little craftsmanship and none of the rust-resisting qualities of iron.

But it was cast iron that the Victorians really loved. It could be cheaply produced and once a pattern was made a design could be easily mass produced. The designers and craftsmen of cast iron products seem to have particularly enjoyed themselves when it came to the manufacture of decorative garden furniture. In

13.   Wrought iron seat, Charlecote, Warwickshire

addition to the romance and intricacy achieved in these designs, cast iron has proved itself to be an ideal material for garden furniture.   It is very resistant to corrosion and its weight prevents gusty summer gales from playing havoc with tables and chairs in the open.   One can see today cast iron plates and notices on canal bridges for instance, where the rust is only a surface coating, the main body of the casting being as sound as when first made some two hundred years ago.

By the nature of its manufacture cast iron products must be thicker and will therefore have a more solid appearance than wrought ironwork.   Because of this, cast iron furniture will stand out more as an 'eye-catching' feature in the garden, particularly if it is painted white and placed against a dark background of shrubs or trees.

The round tables produced by the thousand for the Victorian public house and gin palace, and for clubs, restaurants and gardens, make most admirable and permanent pieces of furniture for our gardens today (Fig. 23).   Although there were many different forms of decoration for these tables they were all of similar construction, consisting of a circular top of good-quality hardwood or sometimes marble, three cast iron legs bolted together to form at the top a decorated band which was fixed to the underside of the table top; and a cast iron plate or shelf fixed to the legs about two-thirds of the way down.   The motifs for the decoration were numerous and widely varied, and included Britannia and her shield—sometimes with the inscription 'Slavery Abolished'—whilst other patterns had ram's heads, Neptune's head, female figureheads, Greek goddesses, or roses and lotus flowers.   The Coalbrookdale Company even made cast iron chess tables.   Some of the cast iron tables intended more for gardens and conservatories had one central support which curved outwards to form three feet at the bottom and supported the

FIG. 23. Cast iron table

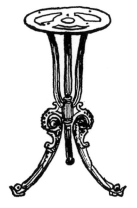

FIG. 24. Cast iron legs
for a garden table

timber top by means of a circular plate (Fig. 24).

English gardens in spring and summer possess a rare and refreshing beauty due largely to their verdant quality produced by a kindly climate. But it is just this climate, so suited to plant growth, that does not always encourage us to take full advantage of outdoor living in the garden. The answer is to follow the example of the Parisian cafés by having tables and chairs permanently placed on the terrace, or in an alcove, so that even on a day with only an hour or two of sunshine one is encouraged to take drinks or meals in the open-air without the laborious task of moving furniture into the garden. Cast iron furniture is particularly suited to being kept permanently, or at least for the summer, in the garden and so offering a constant invitation to be used.

In this country it is possible to buy good examples of public house tables from a number of dealers who specialise in garden ornament and furniture. Alternatively one can, as the author has done on a number of occasions, save from the scrap iron merchant tables and seats that with a little restoration and painting can soon give pleasure and use in the garden. Broken cast iron legs can usually be welded together and timber table tops or seat slats can be easily replaced where necessary. The ironwork seat slats should be properly cleaned and painted—preferably white—and the timber table top cleaned and polished or treated with linseed oil. Should the top be made of marble then but for an unfortunate breakage it will last for ever and become a family heirloom.

Seats had as many different motifs of decoration as public house tables, but were made in many more varied shapes and sizes. Some could be completely made of cast iron (Plate 14)

whilst others would just have cast iron ends with the seat and back composed of timber slats. A most attractive type fairly frequently found is the one made of fern fronds (Plate 15), which always looks well in a courtyard or patio garden. The pattern of fern fronds will cast equally pleasing shadows on to the paving of the courtyard garden. This was the seat that Mr. Holger Blom, the Director of the Parks Department of Stockholm, had copied and which now graces so many of the city's parks and public places. The decoration for the garden seat in the 19th century invariably kept to Gothic and rustic forms. With the Gothic seat quatrefoil shapes and pointed arches predominated (Plate 14).

Rustic ornamentation was all the vogue in the late-Victorian and Edwardian periods of garden design. In ironwork it was common to imitate vine stems complete with leaves and bunches of grapes. The 'Victorian' all cast iron seat (Fig. 25) which is still manufactured by George Lister and Son Ltd. of Cambridge, has this form of decoration and is a delightful and genuine piece of 19th-century garden furniture design that is particularly suited to our small gardens today.

Seats for larger gardens and public parks and promenades in the

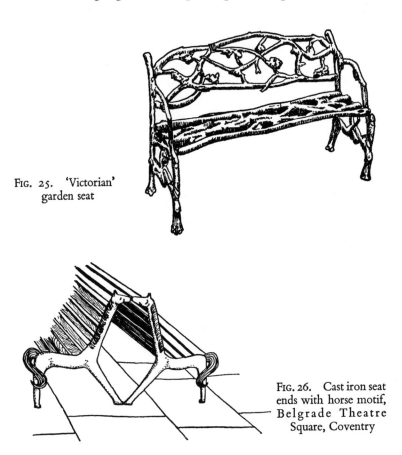

FIG. 25. 'Victorian' garden seat

FIG. 26. Cast iron seat ends with horse motif, Belgrade Theatre Square, Coventry

last century were usually made with cast iron ends and timber slats for the seats and backs. Many towns that were favourite Victorian resorts had seat ends made in the form of serpents and many of these exist today. The serpent was ingeniously shaped to support the seat with its tail forming the back rest. Unfortunately these very sculptural seat ends are too often ignored today. If only they could be cleaned each year and given a fresh coat of paint, they would once again add greatly to the interest of the town.

The City of Coventry (designer Mr. J. C. Brown, A.R.I.B.A.) has recently made some similar seats, this time using a representation of Lady Godiva's horse to form the seat ends. This seat has the added advantage of forming a most attractive composition when the two seats are placed back to back, as they are in the garden square of the Belgrade Theatre (Fig. 26). The Furness Railway, which offered '20 Rail, Coach, and Steam Yacht Tours Through Lakeland,' matched its picturesque setting with a delightful seat especially manufactured for use at its stations and pierheads. The seat ends were beautifully cast into vine stems and grapes which framed a full-sized lakeland squirrel. The author was fortunate enough to purchase one of these seats from British Railways when the Eskmeals Station was recently closed, and now that it is painted white it forms a useful and attractive feature in the garden (Plate 16). Many of these seats are, however, still performing their original purpose on this charming railway at the stations and at the piers serving the lake ferry boats.

It is interesting to find that some firms still have patterns for decorative seat ends. The Bo'ness Iron Co. Ltd., of Bo'ness, Scotland, for instance still offer a selection of twelve different types of cast iron garden seat ends. Many of these designs are similar to those that can be seen in many of our public parks and promenades throughout Britain. Seven of the Bo'ness seats illustrated in the firm's current catalogue have arm rests, and vary from the familiar 'Vine' and 'Bramble' patterns (Figs. 27 and 28) to the very simple rustic form shown in Fig. 31 which is often seen on railway stations.

Individual garden seats or chairs manufactured in metal in the 19th century were often made surprisingly comfortable. The main framework would be manufactured in cast or wrought iron and the seats made with some form of flexible metal. Bands of sheet steel that would have sufficient spring in them to make a comfortable seat and perhaps a back as well were often employed. William Robinson gives an account of these delightful chairs in his book *The Parks, Promenades and Gardens of Paris, Described and Considered in Relation to the Wants of our Cities, . . .*' published in

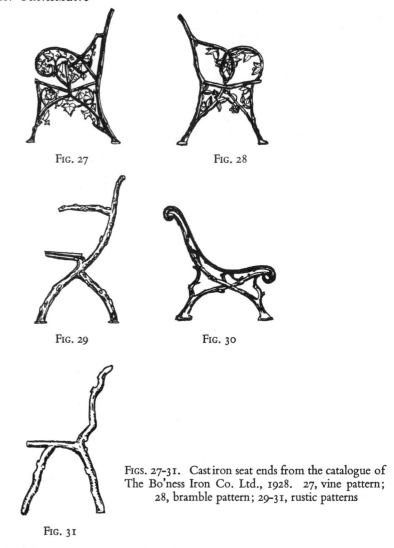

FIG. 27   FIG. 28

FIG. 29   FIG. 30

FIGS. 27-31. Cast iron seat ends from the catalogue of The Bo'ness Iron Co. Ltd., 1928. 27, vine pattern; 28, bramble pattern; 29-31, rustic patterns

FIG. 31

1869. At that time this elegant and comfortable garden seat (Fig. 32) was apparently 'seen in quantities in all public places in Paris'. It was made by M. Carré, of Paris, but similar ones, sometimes with arms, were later manufactured in this country. Robinson was obviously impressed by this excellent piece of garden furniture, and wrote a full description of it in his book. The design had a convex seat made from a number of flexible strips of curved metal bands springing from the seat to a circular centre-piece. The back also had strips of metal bands springing from the seat to a cross member near the top of the back. 'A very neat, elegant, and comfortable conservatory, pleasure ground, or summer-house chair is composed of three of these seats united in one, the larger framework of the back and sides being made of

14.   Cast iron seat, Hidcote Manor, Gloucestershire

15.   Cast iron seat with fern frond pattern, Lanhydrock, Cornwall

rustic iron about as thick as the thumb, the smaller spray being tied to the larger by imitation osier twigs.' The elegance of these garden chairs has today made them very much collectors' pieces, and they are often cherished as fine pieces of furniture for the house, or even used as elegant display props for the shop windows of the more exclusive ladies' dress shops!

Robinson mentioned a similar garden chair made by Tronchon, of the Avenue d'Eylau, 'who has a large collection of such articles'. His modification of Carré's design had interwoven metal bands which again had sufficient spring in them to make it more comfortable than the normal timber slats. From Robinson's description this chair must have looked very similar to the

Fig. 32.   M. Carré's elegant metal garden chair, from William Robinson's *The Parks, Promenades and Gardens of Paris*, 1869

one in the garden at Hidcote Manor, Gloucestershire, which is illustrated on page 67 (Fig. 22).

Wirework was commonly combined with a framework of iron to make some of the most charming Victorian garden furniture. The elegance and intricacy of wirework garden furniture has made most of the surviving examples much sought after today. The wirework, of course, must be regularly painted if it is to survive for long in the garden or even under cover in the conservatory or porch. Most of this furniture was intended for the conservatory or for the verandah. A typical example of the

Fig. 33.   Wirework flower table by Joseph Reynolds, from the 1851 Great Exhibition catalogue

wirework flower table (Fig. 33) was manufactured by Joseph Reynolds, of New Compton Street, London, and was exhibited by that firm at the Great Exhibition of 1851. The table top is supported by three serpents made of wire which unite to form the legs of the table. Flower stands shaped for taking plant pots were also manufactured in a variety of designs (see under Chapter 3 'Sculptured Ornament'). French designers excelled at wirework and Robinson showed in his book *The Parks, Promenades and Gardens of Paris* . . . a particularly beautiful wirework seat (Fig. 34). It was romantically designed to form something of a bower for two persons, for the seat had a box at the back which could be planted with annual climbing plants. This seat was easily movable as its six legs were fitted with castors or small wheels, and 'so shaded and decorated, it might prove very acceptable in some positions' wrote Robinson.

Metal garden furniture in the 19th and early 20th centuries was not restricted only to chairs, seats and tables, but included a

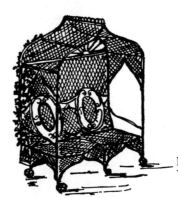

Fig. 34.   Wirework garden seat from William Robinson's *The Parks, Promenades and Gardens of Paris*, 1869

number of miscellaneous furnishings which in the taste of the times were made ornamental as well as functional. Bootscrapers were cast in a variety of ornamental patterns and are now beginning to be a part of the stock of many of the dealers specialising in garden ornaments. The cast iron bootscraper was made either with a long prong by which it was fixed into the ground, or the scraper was movable and was supported from a heavy tray. The prong type frequently had the actual scraper cast in the form of a harp (Fig. 35). Simpler patterns were merely decorated with leaves (Fig. 36). The movable scrapers also had a tray heavy enough to hold the scraper steady whilst it was in use and to collect tidily the falling mud. The decoration of this type of scraper was often based on animal heads (Fig. 37) but there were many other variations. For military households, for instance, the bootscraper could be supported by two crossed cannon (Fig. 38).

In 1896 a garden owner could purchase from Messrs. Boulton and Paul a six-and-a-half-foot-high standard supporting a 'TO THE CONSERVATORY' notice, all cast in iron for the price of forty-three shillings. This must have been a most wonderful status symbol

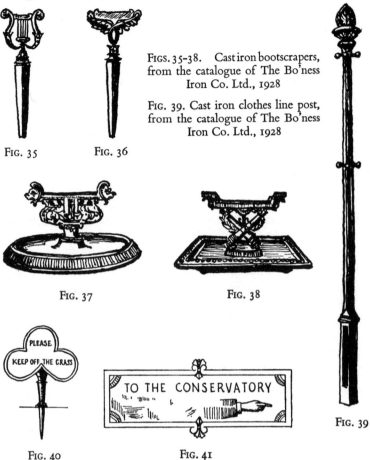

FIGS. 35-38. Cast iron bootscrapers, from the catalogue of The Bo'ness Iron Co. Ltd., 1928

FIG. 39. Cast iron clothes line post, from the catalogue of The Bo'ness Iron Co. Ltd., 1928

FIG. 35   FIG. 36

FIG. 37   FIG. 38

FIG. 40   FIG. 41

FIG. 39

FIG. 40-41. Cast iron garden notices from the 1896 catalogue of Messrs. Boulton and Paul, Ltd.

to have erected in different parts of the garden, always providing that the conservatory could live up to such advance publicity. Even mundane objects such as clothes line posts when manufactured in cast iron had considerable elegance and were suitably topped with a robust finial (Fig. 39). 'PLEASE KEEP OFF THE GRASS' notices when made in cast iron were not without style (Fig. 40). Messrs. Boulton and Paul's catalogue of 1896 showed such a notice elegantly cast in the form of a clover-leaf.

The ridiculous vogue for having oversized and artificial toadstools or mushrooms in the garden had its origins in 19th-century cast iron ornament. The famous early Victorian garden at

Redleaf, Penshurst, had cast iron seats in the shape of giant mushrooms, but they at least then had the function of providing a seat and were not painted in today's lurid colour scheme of red and white polka dots.

One of the annual jobs to be done in the garden in Victorian and Edwardian Britain was the spring cleaning and painting of the garden furniture. Where this is still carried out most people would agree that this small effort is well worth while. It can only be regretted that this annual repainting is not more often carried out. White is undoubtedly the most successful colour to paint all decorative garden furniture (Plate 13) but black is sometimes appropriate for ironwork. Bright colours will usually look lurid and too competitive with the colours of the garden, whilst nothing could be more discordant than the popular 'natural' green which will inevitably clash with the greens of vegetation. Mrs. Loudon and many writers since have advised against painting garden seats green, but the idea that this is a natural colour and therefore should be used in the garden is still strongly held by too many gardeners.

With seats and table tops constructed in good-quality hardwood, painting will not be necessary, unless the seat is of a very pleasing shape and would be more effectively displayed by being painted white. In the 19th century stone was a highly regarded material and like most highly regarded things it was frequently imitated. Stucco on buildings, for instance, was originally painted to look like stonework. Similarly garden seats were constructed to resemble stone ones and were often painted with a mixture of stone-coloured paint and sand to help the illusion.

The popularity of the Italian-style formal garden in England in the middle of the 19th century created a demand for stone or marble benches in the classical style. A number were simple stone benches with the ends decorated with scrolls or lions' heads. A favourite feature to terminate a formal terrace or to decorate a niche in the neo-Italian garden was the semi-circular stone or marble seat (Fig. 42) which although hardly inviting except on the hottest days in our climate, did have a stately air of grandeur

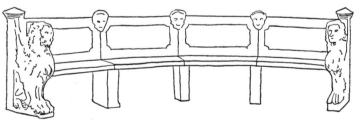

FIG. 42. Semi-circular stone seat in the Italian style

and permanence.   Most of these Italian-style gardens have now disappeared, but their substantial ornaments, including the stone seats, are often to be found in the yards of dealers selling garden ornaments.

19th-century Britain saw a number of major social upheavals. The most important change affecting the garden was the growth of the middle classes, that in a comparatively short space of time gave rise to countless villa gardens in the new and fashionable suburbs around all our industrial centres and in the new towns catering for retirement or illness.   Many of these middle-class men were also employed in running the vast British Empire. Steam power harnessed in ships and on the railways transported not only the administrators but also their families to and fro between the mother country and the far-flung Empire.   The Victorian middle classes with their love for comfort in furniture soon invented or adapted furniture to make the long sea voyages more pleasurable.   The most important piece of new furniture, so far as the garden was concerned, was the steamer chair (Fig. 43) introduced in the late 1850's.   It was the forerunner of today's ubiquitous deck-chair, and remained a popular garden chair throughout the second half of the 19th century.   The outstanding

FIG. 43.   Steamer chair

feature of the steamer chair was that it could be folded up and stowed away when not in use, either in the lockers of the steam-ship or in the garden summer-house.   It had elegance and like

most Victorian furniture it was comfortable, especially when it was equipped with sumptuous cushions—which was often the case judging from contemporary illustrations.   The steamer chair had six legs and the seat, and usually the back, were made from inter-woven split cane.   Some had a detachable leg-rest which not only added to the comfort of lounging in the chair but could make it into a useful day bed.   The type made in mahogany with a slatted back and cane seat was called a Derby folding chair.

Frailer materials than stone, iron, or wood have been used in the construction of furniture for covered parts of the garden.   Straw seats shaped like half-beehives were marketed in the 19th century and must have been very snug.   Osier wickerwork and cane were greatly favoured in the early part of the 20th century for garden chairs and tables that were placed on the verandah, and in the conservatory and summer-house.   Many delightful shapes have been evolved for wickerwork chairs together with a number of matching accessories.   Where tables and chairs are to be used frequently for open-air meals it is particularly attractive if the necessary equipment of trays, china or pottery is in harmony with the furniture.   Obviously, delicate china will look out of place with unsophisticated rustic furniture.

The choice of ornamental garden seats today is not confined to the dealer in antique or Victorian garden furniture, but includes a number of manufacturers producing designs either in past styles or in the modern idiom.   Within these two groups there are both good and bad examples.   The manufacturer using genuine Victorian or Regency cast iron patterns and using iron for the castings will produce a seat that is in no way inferior to a similar example preserved or restored from a 19th-century garden.   The least satisfactory are those that are made in imitation of cast iron, when for instance thin aluminium mimics solid iron castings. These substitutes in aluminium alloys make a mockery of the original robust cast iron design and look altogether sham.

The traditional and very beautiful wrought iron seat can still be made by a skilled blacksmith where he is building to a good design and is really working in wrought iron.   All too often, however, welded and bent mild steel is made to imitate, and is even called, wrought iron.   The result is a silly sham and should be avoided.

One of the most elegant of contemporary designs for cast iron garden seats is the one by Edward Bawden (Fig. 44), the Aca-demician who has never been afraid of using decoration in his designs for contemporary pottery, wallpapers, and textiles.[1] The original Bawden seat has now been adapted to a chair and

[1] This range of cast iron seats designed by Bawden is manufactured by Bilston Foundries Ltd.

16.   A Furness Railway seat in author's garden

table design, so that a complete range of these gay and decorative pieces of garden furniture is now available.

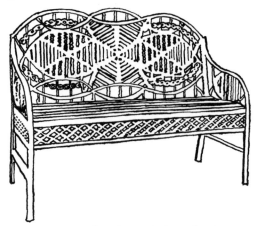

FIG. 44.   Edward Bawden's garden seat

But the vast majority of today's well-designed examples of garden furniture are devoid of decoration and rely on their shape and form for their visual appeal.   Traditional materials such as thick wire or cane with steel frames are still popular with designers whilst a larger range of visually less pleasing chairs made from aluminium alloy frames and canvas or plastic upholstery are in the majority.   However, some recent designs in aluminium alloy frames have combined elegance with comfort.   The folding deck-chair still remains a good-selling garden chair, and recently a contemporary deck-chair originally designed for use aboard ship has been put on the market as a garden chair.   This contemporary deck-chair has the back and seat in two units and is therefore better able to support the user.   The frame is made in afrormosia and the seat and back is in resin-bonded formed plywood with afrormosia veneers.[1]

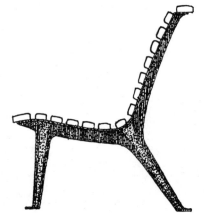

FIG. 45.   LM outdoor seat

[1] Manufactured by Race Furniture Ltd.

Today's designers of seats or benches for public places also follow the common trend of avoiding decoration.   The most successful of these designs depend therefore on good shape and proportion, fitness for purpose and of course, the minimum requirements for maintenance.   A good example of this type of modern seat is the LM Outdoor Seat.[1]   Fig. 45 shows that this LM seat is not only elegant in outline but that it is shaped so that it will properly support the human frame in a sitting position. The LM seat has a heavy cast iron frame which is stove-enamelled black to give a tough finish requiring little in the way of maintenance.   The slats for the seat and back are made from afrormosia which except for occasional oiling requires no maintenance.   The feet can have holes cast in them to take bolts which can be fixed into concrete set in the ground.   This seat is manufactured in two lengths: an eight-foot one with six legs and a six-foot three-inch one with six or four legs.   The LM Outdoor Seats are undoubtedly well designed for minimum maintenance, elegance and comfort, and where decoration is not required these seats have proved themselves to be a good piece of contemporary design.   A new range known as the 1010 seats has recently been brought out by this firm and includes a single-seater armchair made from heavy mild steel square section tubes and oiled afrormosia slats. This range is claimed to be 'as hooligan proof as seems humanly possible', as the steel sections are very substantial and the bolts are

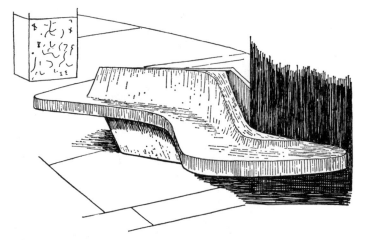

FIG. 46.   Heated concrete seat at Stockholm

all countersunk and the nuts riveted during assembly to discourage idle dismantlers.

Seats made entirely of timber are perhaps the commonest type of outdoor seat manufactured today.   But the majority of them

[1] Manufactured by LM Furniture Ltd.

are poorly designed, possessing neither elegance nor much in the way of comfort. Better designs have appeared in recent years for timber chairs with matching tables which will make a pleasing group in a garden corner.

Reinforced concrete for the supports for seats is frequently used today, especially for benches for public use. Concrete has the merit of not requiring any maintenance, and can be readily fixed into the ground and so foil some forms of vandalism. With adequate reinforcement and good-quality concrete the actual seat can be easily carried out as a cantilever from the main support, providing, of course, that the support is securely anchored into the ground. This arrangement has been used in the design of the Mayfair seat.[1] The concrete can be given a variety of finishes such as exposed aggregate. Charming concrete seats faced with mosaic have been used in public gardens in Brazil, where the plastic quality of concrete has been exploited to allow the seat to follow the serpentine line of the mosaic or tile paving. But cold materials such as concrete and mosaic are only suited to hot climates, unless of course the principle of local heating is applied to the seat. This has been done in the case of the heated platform seat on the underground railway in Stockholm (Fig. 46). The seat stands in the open, and is a shapely structure made in reinforced concrete in which are embedded half-inch-diameter copper hot-water pipes. The pipes connect to the general heating system from the buildings below the platform, and so provides local heating for waiting passengers in the winter months.

[1] Manufactured by Mono Concrete Co. Ltd.

17.   Armillary sundial, Woburn Abbey, Bedfordshire

Chapter Three

SCULPTURED ORNAMENT

*Sundials; carved heraldic beasts; lead figures; lead vases, urns,
cisterns, etc.; Italian garden figures; artificial stonework; cast
and wrought iron ornaments; wirework; bird-baths; gnomes and
toadstools; sculpture; murals; rocks and boulders.*

GARDEN design before the 18th century was invariably based on a formal geometric plan. The garden would be enclosed by walls or hedges and an ornamental feature would be centrally placed at the meeting-point of several paths. At first, this centrepiece was commonly a well-head or a fountain providing drinking water from a near-by spring, but by the 16th century the sundial, supported on an ornamental pedestal or column, was becoming a more popular garden feature. Just as the well-head had originally been provided as a functional object for the manor house or monastery, so too was the sundial placed in the garden for a utilitarian purpose; in this case to measure time. In the 16th century clocks were still very expensive and something of a rarity, so that sundials were the most commonly used instrument for the measurement of time, and even when there was a clock, the sundial provided the best means of checking on its accuracy.

Sundials had of course been used for many centuries before they were placed in the garden. Before the 16th century, sundials in Britain had been carved and painted on to walls of religious foundations and manor houses. The earliest known shadow-clock is an Egyptian one which dates from about 1500 B.C., a fragment of which is in the British Museum. It is thought that obelisks were originally used as primitive time-tellers in Egypt. The sundial was used throughout the Greek and Roman Empires, and several Saxon examples are still in existence in this country.

The best masons were expected to be able to make a sundial and the leading mathematicians were often employed on the lineating of important and complicated dials, whilst some of the finest craftsmen were called upon to engrave the bronze or copper plates. Many ingenious devices for telling the time from the sun were invented. One such invention, although rather uncommon, was the reflective dial. This consisted of a small circular mirror fixed to a window-sill or floor which reflected the sun's rays on to the ceiling of the room, which was painted with hour lines and numerals. Sir Isaac Newton designed for himself a sundial of this type.

There was also a more spectacular cannon sundial which used the sun to fire a charge, usually arranged for noon. A cannon dial of French manufacture, and dated 1782, can be seen in the Science Museum, London. This example has a lens on an adjustable arm which can be so arranged as to focus the image of the sun on the touch-hole of the cannon at noon. The cannon was employed in the 19th and early 20th centuries on plantations in India to signal to workers the time for rest. One of the earliest

FIG. 47.   Column sundial,
Corpus Christi College,
Oxford, 1605

the 18th century.   This dial has four prancing lions standing back to back and each holding a dial face and gnomon.   The lions are also supporting a large block of stone which has been cut into no less than eighty triangular planes on which further gnomons are fixed.   The pillar is crowned by a coronet.   The lions are from the arms of the Strathmore family who still own Glamis Castle.

At Kelburne Castle, Ayrshire, there are two fine sundials consisting of tapering four-sided columns crowned in one case by a vane (Fig. 48) and dated 1707, and in the other by a stone ball.

FIG. 48.   Early 18th-century column
sundial, Kelburne Castle, Ayrshire

surviving examples of a free-standing garden sundial is the one in the quadrangle of Corpus Christi College, Oxford (Fig. 47). It has five dials, one of which is concave; four coats of arms as well as four mottoes, which are surmounted by a globe and a pelican— the crest of the college.   This elaborate structure was erected in 1605 by Charles Turnbull, a fellow of the college.   It was said to have been regarded as 'inconvenient' during the time of the threatened invasion by Napoleon, when the quadrangle was used as a drilling ground, but fortunately it was not removed and remains today as a memorial to Turnbull's mathematical skill.

In the 17th and 18th centuries the cubic multiheaded sundial was popular, particularly in Scotland where many of these elaborate dials can be seen today.   Queen Mary's dial at Holyroodhouse is of this period.   It was originally placed in the formal layout in the King's Privy Garden, but now stands near the James IV Tower.   This sundial was presented to Henrietta Maria by Charles I and cost £408.   It was made in 1633 by the King's Master Mason John Mylne, assisted by his sons, Alexander and John.   It consists of a block of stone cut into many planes and concave dial faces, which is supported by a stone column that rises from three steps.

There is a very elaborate sundial at Glamis Castle, Angus, which was made at the beginning of the 17th century and was not swept away in Capability Brown's landscape improvements in

The dials are on vertical planes.   Good examples of a cubic sundial with several heads can be seen at Drummond Castle, Perthshire, Melville House, Fifeshire, and at many other famous Scottish gardens.

The King's Privy Garden in Whitehall seems to have had a number of grand sundials.   Nicholas Stone, the sculptor, made one for this garden in 1622 to the design of Edmund Gunter, Professor of Astrology at Gresham College.   It had a great many dials including a great concave one in the middle.   It was one of Charles I's most cherished possessions.   But none was quite so fantastic as the pyramidal dial erected in 1669 for Charles II in the Privy Garden at Whitehall.   It had 271 different dials and showed the time according to the Jewish, Babylonian, Italian and astronomical ways of counting, as well as much information relating to astronomy, geography, and astrology. The designer was the Rev. Francis Hall, alias Lyne, a professor of mathematics at Liège, where he had also erected a similar dial. By all accounts it was not an object of beauty, nor was it constructed to withstand weathering in the open, for in 1710 William Allingham, a mathematician in Cannon Row, asked £500 to repair this sundial.

A type of sundial that became popular in the 18th century, and has been a much favoured ornament for the garden ever since, was the Armillary or Horological Sphere (Plate 17). The true armillary sphere is not a sundial at all but an astronomical instrument used before the birth of Christ in China and in Greece. The sphere consists of a number of rings revolving around each other about the earth or the sun. The rings represented the more important circles of the celestial spheres. The instrument was probably used more as a model for teaching purposes than for practical astronomy. One of the finest armillary spheres in Britain is the one in the Bodleian Library, Oxford, which was made at the end of the 16th century. It is two feet in diameter, made of bronze, and is supported by three lions crouching on a triangular base. The armillary sundial is similar in appearance to the astronomical instrument, having metal rings—one of which represents the equator—which are pierced by an arrow representing the earth's axis. When well designed and executed it is a most decorative sundial, for the lightness and elegance of the

18. Scheemaker's Dying Gladiator, Rousham, Oxfordshire

sphere makes a pleasing contrast with the solid base or pedestal by which it is normally supported. The armillary sphere sundial, where it has a base properly in scale with its setting, will make a most pleasing centre-piece to the formal garden.

One of the most realistic, although rather rare, types of sundial is the stone ball arrangement, where the ball represents the earth, and the time is indicated on the ball at the point where the light and shadow meet.

The majority of sundials were simply a horizontal plate engraved with hour-lines, numerals and probably a motto, with a projecting shadow arm or gnomon running parallel with the earth's axis. The horizontal dial or plate should be made from a metal that can be engraved but which will not easily be corroded, such as brass, bronze or copper. But cheaper materials have been used including in the 19th century cast iron, which from the point of view of accurately telling the time on a small dial is unsatisfactory, due to the lack of precision in iron casting. The free-standing horizontal dial is usually supported by a column or baluster, but occasionally by a sculptured figure such as the famous lead blackamoor which was so popular in the 17th and 18th centuries.

FIG. 49. Baluster-type sundial. Hampton Court, Middlesex

Some of the most beautiful garden sundials have been the simplest, where the proportions of the baluster and the engraving of the plate have been perfectly designed and executed. A fine example of this is the baluster-type sundial at Hampton Court (Fig. 49) designed in the style of Christopher Wren.

Mottoes are very much associated with sundials. They are either engraved on the plate or carved on the structure. Many of the mottoes comment on the passing of time, and man's short life span in such discomforting lines as:

Time wastes us all, our bodies and our wits;
But we waste time, so time and we are quits

or

Man fleeth as a shadow

or

Ut Umbra Sic Vita (As a shadow, so is life)

Mrs. Alfred Gatty in the 19th century collected several hundred different mottoes used on sundials and published these in her famous work *The Book of Sun-dials*. They include mottoes for all moods and situations from such salutations as:

Amicis Qualibet Hora (To Friends—any hour they please)

to the graceful and appropriate appeal:

Aspice Ut Aspiciar (Look on me that I may be looked on)

A popular theme for mottoes is to give advice on getting out of bed in the morning and stressing the successes awaiting in life for those who rise early.

He that would thrive must rise at five,
He that hath thriven may stay till seven
He that will never thrive may stay till eleven.

Sundials in the garden must, of course, be placed in an open position away from shadows cast by trees or buildings. As it will be seen from a number of positions, it is most essential that the supporting base or column should be well proportioned and present a good appearance from any direction.

A sundial when properly set up indicates the apparent solar time of the place. There are only a few days of the year when the sundial agrees with the local mean time. To obtain the local mean time of the place one has to refer to a table giving the equation of time, which gives how many minutes the watch is slow or fast of sun time for each day of the year. This table is given in most nautical almanacs, and shows that the watch can be up to sixteen minutes slow or up to fourteen minutes fast of sun time. The equation of time was first worked out in the 17th century, and since that time many sundials have a graduated circle of dates giving the corresponding equation of time—how many minutes the clock is fast or slow of sun time. Many clocks in the 17th and 18th centuries also showed the equation of time, usually a month at a time, so that the accuracy of the clock could be checked with the sundial. Today, of course, we no longer use local mean time, but use instead Greenwich Mean Time.

In the 'new and enlarged edition' of Mrs. Alfred Gatty's *The Book of Sun-dials* edited by H. K. F. Gatty and Eleanor Lloyd, published in 1889, there is a useful appendix written by W.

19.   18th-century lead figure of a shepherd, Charlecote,
Warwickshire

Richardson on the actual construction of horizontal and wall sundials. The appendix includes diagrams which it was hoped would 'be useful in cases where a vicar or his churchwardens are willing to restore an old relic, but do not know how to make the calculations necessary for doing so'. For more unusual dials the reader was referred to *Treatise on Dialling* by Peter Nicholson, published in Newcastle on Tyne in 1833; and *Dialling* by William Leybourn, published by A. and J. Churchill in 1700.

In the 16th and 17th centuries the favourite colour scheme for painting dials was blue with the hour lines picked out in gold. These colours are undoubtedly the most appropriate and pleasing scheme for painting dials today.

Sculpture in gardens was first used in as prominent a way as possible. In some Tudor and Elizabethan gardens the sculpture often appears to have completely dominated the rest of the garden. More generally sculpture would be placed at the junction of paths, at the ends of alleyways and vistas, or sited so as to emphasise important places such as entrances where figures or other ornaments would be fixed on to gate piers, or by flights of steps, or to decorate the tops of walls and terrace balustrades. With the changes brought about by the invention of picturesque landscape gardening in the 18th century, the only ornaments in scale with the larger views and prospects were buildings. Sculpture was then either banished altogether from the garden or partly hidden in groves or placed in the new garden buildings. With the return to fashion of formal gardening in the second half of the 19th century, sculpture and other ornaments became again a more prominent element in the garden scene. Whilst nearer the present day, the naturalistic style of gardening as taught by William Robinson in his book *The Wild Garden* published in 1870, and later in his more famous and influential book *The English Flower Garden and Home Grounds* first published in 1883, found little space for ornaments, except on the terrace, in the courtyard, and occasionally, but always discreetly, in some woodland glade.

Sculpture and ornaments have always been thought appropriate for the small enclosed garden and the courtyard, for this is where a dominating and eye-catching feature is most needed and most effective. Today's gardens are smaller and more like courtyard gardens if not actually built as patios, and this no doubt has helped to promote the present keen demand for small pieces of statuary, urns, lead cisterns, and ornamental iron seats.

Some of the earliest sculpture made for English gardens were carved and painted heraldic animals. These were carved throughout the 16th century for the more notable and splendid gardens

of the time. Henry VIII, after he had taken over Hampton Court from Cardinal Wolsey, considerably enlarged the gardens, and gave orders for the making of a large number of carved and painted animals. In 1910 some of Henry VIII's heraldic supporters of the King's arms were excavated from the old filled-in moat. They were then repaired and are now once again on view (Fig. 50). Queen Elizabeth I also had her privy garden in Whitehall decorated with some thirty-four heraldic beasts, with most of them supporting aloft vanes painted with royal arms.

The heraldic figures carved in stone which were placed in front of the great window of the Annexe of Westminster Abbey for the coronation of Her Majesty Queen Elizabeth II in 1953 had much of the spirit and form of their Tudor counterparts. Ten of these figures, each with shields, were copied in Portland stone by the

FIG. 50. One of Henry VIII's heraldic supporters, Hampton Court, Middlesex

same sculptor, Mr. James Woodford, and can be seen today on the terrace of the Palm House at the Royal Botanic Gardens, Kew.

But gardens such as Hampton Court were exceptional and it was not until the 17th century that sculpture and sculptors were to be commonly employed in the decoration of gardens. It was the new formal gardens at Wilton House, Wiltshire, laid out by Isaac de Caus in the early 17th century, that started the more widespread use of garden statuary, waterworks, and ornaments in gardens in this country. The style of this garden and its decoration owed more to the growing influence of the Renaissance than to the mediaeval world of knot gardens, mounds, arbours, and heraldic decoration.

After the Restoration the influence of the Renaissance from the Continent, in particular from Italy and France, completely dominated the arts of architecture and gardening in Britain. In gardening, the famous parks and gardens laid out by that celebrated French landscape designer, André le Nôtre, notably at Vaux-le-Vicomte and at Versailles, had the greatest direct influence in the second half of the 17th century. Versailles was laid out during the years 1667 to 1688, although le Nôtre worked on the layout on and off throughout the rest of his life. The gardens were on an enormous scale, covering with the park some 24,000 acres, and were at the time the admiration and envy of the Western world. Everywhere nature was subjected to the laws of symmetry and formality. The ground was levelled into terraces, water arranged into formal basins or canals, trees planted in plantations of geometric shapes, and vegetation trained, clipped, and otherwise arranged into abstract shapes and patterns. Sculpture was most plentiful, for nearly one hundred sculptors under the direction of le Brun and Mignard were employed by Louis XIV to decorate the grounds. Many of these works were destroyed in the French Revolution, but enough have survived to give the visitor to the gardens today an impression of great abundance of statuary and sculptured fountain groups. The subjects for sculpture, if the work did not have to commemorate one of the King's victories on the battlefield, would include actual copies from the antique, figures from classical mythology, such as cupids, Bacchus, many figures of Apollo, meant as 'flattering allusions to the Roi-Soleil'—Louis XIV—and river gods and nymphs for watery places. All these subjects for sculpture were soon to be considered most appropriate for parks and gardens in Britain in the late 17th century and throughout the 18th century.

But the influence of the Renaissance on the arts in this country came not only via France but also from the Low Countries. In 1688 Princess Mary and her husband William of Orange were invited to leave Holland and to come to England with an army to rescue the country from 'popery and slavery'. They accepted the invitation and landed at Torbay. So many people flocked to give support to William that James II was forced to flee from the country and take refuge at the Court of his cousin Louis XIV. William and Mary were proclaimed and crowned in 1668. Their rule naturally brought about closer ties with protestant Europe, and in particular with Holland. French culture as epitomised by the Court of Louis XIV was considered undemo-cratic, dictatorial and altogether lacking in freedom by the majority of Englishmen. Throughout the reign of William and Mary, Dutch influence in the sciences and arts was most important, and many of our ideas in agriculture, land-draining, navigation, commerce, painting, sculpture, architecture, and gardening were to come from Holland. In building it brought about a greater use of brickwork, so masterfully used by Sir Christopher Wren in conjunction with Portland stone in the design of domestic houses, whilst in gardening many of the new fashions in the late 17th century came from Holland, notably clipped alleyways, mostly in yew, pleached limes, topiary and charming lead figures. The Dutch garden was more intimate than the French park or garden which relied on vast vistas and huge terraces for its appeal. The Dutch style divided the grounds into a series of compartments by means of hedges or walls; the latter having beautifully wrought iron grilles and entrance gates which gave glimpses of the luxurious scene within.

Dutch gardens always contained a number of statues and ornaments in lead. Lead, of course, could be cast and was therefore capable of repetition, and would also withstand the eroding forces of the weather. Not only did the fashion for using lead ornaments in the garden come from the Low Countries, but many of the designers and manufacturers also came from this part of Europe.

Any work on the history of garden ornament must give an account of these sculptors, for this is the finest period for garden sculpture in Britain. Later periods have produced a larger quantity of ornaments but never of such a consistently high standard. Perhaps it was the combination of artist and manufacturer being the one firm, together with the high standard of taste prevailing amongst their patrons, that contributed most to bringing about this happy state of garden ornament. Mass-produced garden ornament today has still to receive the attention of designers of the quality that worked on garden statuary in the 17th and 18th centuries.

The first sculptor in this long line of artists executing works for the garden was Gabriel Cibber (1630-1670), who was born in Fensborg, Holstein, a son of the King of Denmark's cabinet-maker. Soon after arriving in England he worked for John Stone, an English sculptor, but eventually was appointed carver to the King's closet. This appointment seems to have given him little work, for most of his commissions came from private sources. The first Duke of Devonshire employed him at Chatsworth, where he carved many stone figures for the garden between 1689 and 1691. Many of these figures have decayed and have been replaced by Italian-made figures carved in Carrara

20.   Stone urn, Woburn Abbey, Bedfordshire

marble which although more resistant to weathering and decay look too stark and clinical for English gardens. Those that survive to this day include the figures for the Triton Fountain (originally in the parterre on the West Front, but now at one end of the Canal), the Sea-horse Fountain, the statue of Flora, and two winged sphinxes placed on tall pedestals which originally formed a part of Tijou's palisade on the West Front. In the chapel Cibber executed the two statues one on either side of the altar, representing Faith and Hope. Cibber also worked at Hampton Court, but surviving works have now been transferred to Windsor Castle; these include the large marble vase, and statues of Flora, Pomona, Ceres and Diana. Many of Cibber's works elsewhere have eroded away, but a statue of Charles II carved by Cibber still stands in the open in Soho Square, where the plaque spells his name Kibber.

Working at the same time as Cibber was Arnold Quellin (1653-1686), son of the famous Antwerp family of sculptors. He was employed to carve figures for many of the City Companies of London. Although he is known to have executed garden ornaments for Carlton, County Kildare (see *Country Life*, November, 1936), he is mostly remembered, so far as the garden is concerned, as giving employment to John Van Nost (1688-1729), after he had arrived in England from Mechelen, near Antwerp. After Quellin's death Van Nost married his master's widow and so took over the business which he developed into one of the most successful suppliers of lead garden figures.

One of John Van Nost's earliest patrons was Thomas Coke of Melbourne Hall, Derbyshire, where the garden had been laid out in the formal style between 1704 and 1711 by Henry Wise, the leading garden designer of the time. Such a layout needed a plentiful supply of sculpture, and Van Nost was soon called in to provide much of this ornament. One of the finest of Van Nost's works at Melbourne is the lead Vase of the Seasons, which is placed at the meeting of several avenues. It was made in 1705, and then cost £100. Other works by Van Nost at Melbourne include two pairs of amorini, statues of Perseus, Andromeda, Mercury, and Syca (Psyche), and two kneeling figures, one an Indian, the other a blackamoor. The blackamoor became a popular figure and many castings were made for other gardens, and several are still in existence. It consisted of a kneeling negro supporting a sundial on his head. Many of the lead figures at Castle Howard, Yorkshire, are thought to be by Van Nost as are the lead figures near the cascade pools at Rousham, Oxfordshire.

After Van Nost's death in 1729 the business was taken over by his nephew John Van Nost, the Younger, who continued pro-ducing lead figures from this workshop until 1750 when he moved to Dublin and there became the leading sculptor in Ireland.

A fellow countryman of John Van Nost the Elder was Peter Scheemakers (1691-1770), who first came to fame with his finely carved statue of Shakespeare in Westminster Abbey. He executed important works, principally in stone and in marble, for some of the most celebrated gardens of the 18th century. At Stowe he was responsible for the figures of Lycurgus, Socrates, Homer, and Epainondas, a bust of Richard Grenville, Earl Temple (the owner of Stowe), and a colossal statue of George II. With his fellow countryman Laurent Delvaux he carried out in marble two groups of Vertumnus and Pomona, and Venus and Adonis, executed it was said as a trial of their mastery of sculpture. Many of his statues were of figures from the ancient world—heroic subjects for heroic landscapes—such as the Dying Gladiator carved in stone (Plate 18) reclining on William Kent's arcaded terrace called the Praeneste[1] at Rousham.

Also working at the same time as Scheemakers were the brothers Cheere. The elder brother Henry (later knighted for his work) was probably a pupil of Van Nost and was for some time in partnership with Scheemakers. His workshop and yard at Hyde Park Corner became a most prolific supplier of lead garden ornament and was quite famous in its day. Coleman and Garrick in their comedy *Clandestine Marriage* referred to him as 'the man from Hyde Park Corner'. Sir Henry Cheere was born in 1703, retired from business in 1770 and died in 1781. His brother John was first in partnership with Henry, but later took over Van Nost's yard together with his moulds for lead figures in about 1739. There were therefore professional connections between the Van Nosts, Scheemakers, and the brothers Cheere, which no doubt accounts for some of the uncertainty as to who designed and executed many of the lead figures dating from about this time. Powis Castle near Welshpool, Montgomeryshire, and now National Trust property, is a case in point. The terrace gardens here were laid out between 1690 and 1722 by the earls of Rochford, a Dutch family, who naturally also had a Dutch water garden constructed. The Dutch garden contained a lead statue of Fame mounted on Pegasus which now stands in the forecourt of the castle. On the terraces and throughout the garden there are many statues and urns all cast in lead said to have been mined from the rich lead deposits on the estate. The four figures of shepherds and shepherdesses are either the work of the Cheere brothers or Van Nost, but as the same moulds were used by both workshops it is impossible to be more precise. A similar shepherd

[1] Named after the hill town south of Rome.

21.   Bronze urn modelled by Louis Ballin, goldsmith to Louis
XIV, Lanhydrock House, Cornwall

and shepherdess (Plate 19) can be seen in the forecourt at Charle-cote, Warwickshire, also owned by the National Trust, and in several other gardens throughout the country.

The popular subjects for these figures would be of a less heroic character than those chosen by the stone carvers like Scheemakers. Contemporary writers mention casts for such rustic figures as haymakers with rakes; mowers whetting their scythes; game-keepers in the act of shooting; shepherds and shepherdesses; bag-pipers and ordinary pipers, and fiddlers. Pantomime figures were popular, such as Punch, Harlequin, and Columbine, as also were Dutch skippers, English sailors, Father Time with a scythe, piping fauns, the kneeling blackamoor supporting a sundial, the Four Seasons, and even Roman soldiers with firelocks! At the time it was the custom to paint in several colours many of these figures, and occasionally this is still carried out.

Quite a number of fine pieces of sculpture for gardens are attributed to John Cheere. For Bowood, Wiltshire, between 1762 and 1763 he cast in lead the fine figures of Apollo, Venus, Mercury, Liva, Augusta, and Flora, and also busts of Fortina and Antinous. At Blenheim he was responsible for the sphinxes on the bridge, and at Stourhead he supplied lead statues of Pomona, Minerva, Urania, Venus, Mercury, Apollo, and Bacchus, as well as classical figures for the Pantheon garden building and the splendid river god in the grotto. The latter figure is often attributed to Rysbrack, but Rupert Gunnis in his *Dictionary of British Sculptors, 1660-1851*, gives conclusive evidence that this was in fact the work of John Cheere.

The most famous of Cheere's pupils was the Frenchman, Louis François Roubiliac (1695-1762), who came to London in 1738. Roubiliac had the good fortune to find a valuable pocket-book belonging to Horace Walpole's brother Edward. From this chance happening Edward took a interest in the unknown artist and recommended him to Cheere as a pupil. Roubiliac's most notable work is the statue of Handel, which for many years was one of the most admired works of art in London's Vauxhall Pleasure Gardens. With the aid of a grant from the National Art Collection Fund it has recently been bought by the Victoria and Albert Museum.

Another sculptor from the Low Countries—he was born in Antwerp—who worked in England about this time was Michael Rysbrack (1696-1770). Rysbrack was perhaps the greatest sculptor working in 18th-century England. He was a friend of many important artists of the time including the architects James Gibb and William Kent and also of the influential poet Alexander Pope. Much of Rysbrack's work was for the great landscape

FIG. 51. Temple of British Worthies, Stowe, Buckinghamshire

gardens being created at that time. His work consisted mostly of individual commissions, rather than for the more mass-produced castings that came from his contemporaries' workshops. Some of his best work for gardens was for Henry Hoare at Stourhead, notably the nymph in whitened lead in the grotto, the great marble statue of Hercules in the entrance to the Pantheon, the statue of Flora also in the Pantheon, and two statues for the niches beneath the entablature of the Temple of the Sun. At the famous gardens at Stowe, Buckinghamshire, he is reputed to have carved the many busts for the Temple of British Worthies (Fig. 51). For Longford Castle, Wiltshire, he executed the statue of Fame. At Chatsworth in the entrance court there is a fine figure of a recumbent goat carved by Rysbrack which was originally commissioned for the gardens at Chiswick House, but which was moved to Chatsworth when the Duke of Devonshire in 1928 sold his London home to the local council. All of Rysbrack's work is of a high quality and for his work at Stour-head alone he deserves a better remembered place in British sculpture.

The new style of landscape gardening, the picturesque or in-formal, allowed no compromise. The great formal layouts with their terraces, parterres, topiary, avenues, canals, and statuary were swept away to provide a pastoral setting for the house, a setting which is now so universally associated with the typically English country house. The change was not dramatically achieved in a few years, but gradually took place over two or

22. Lead figures of deer in the wild garden, Batsford Park, Gloucestershire

23. Figure in concrete in author's garden. Sculptor, John Bridgeman

three decades in the early part of the 18th century. Consequently the gardens laid out in the first half of the 18th century show a gradual transition from the strictly formal and richly ornamented to the natural landscape park as typified by the work of Capability Brown. In the transitional garden, sculpture still had an important place, but there was less of it and it would be placed only at the end of vistas. Charles Bridgeman's 'new garden' laid out between 1720 and 1725 at Rousham is typical of this period. In fact William Shenstone, an early pioneer of the picturesque landscape wrote in his essay *Unconnected Thoughts on Gardening* 'by the way, I wonder that lead statues are not more in vogue in our modern gardens'. Shenstone was also fond of recommending the use of urns in gardens, particularly because of their melancholy associations, for with the picturesque garden a variety of moods must be contrived for the enjoyment of the owner. 'Urns are more solemn, if large and plain; more beautiful, if less ornamented. Solemnity is perhaps their point, and the situation of them should still operate with it,' wrote Shenstone. Nevertheless, he makes it clear that ornament should not dominate the now natural-looking landscape, and laments the fact that these decorations are more exposed to the general view in the winter. 'To see one's urns, obelisks, and waterfalls laid open; the nakedness of our beloved mistresses, the Naiads, and the Dryads, exposed by that ruffian Winter to universal observation; is a severity scarcely to be supported by the help of blazing hearths, cheerful companions, and a bottle of the most grateful burgundy.'

By the second half of the 18th century most landowners were busily and enthusiastically sweeping away the great formal layouts that existed around their houses and with them went most of the lead statuary. Many of these lead ornaments were uprooted and sold and subsequently melted down to provide bullets for the long and far-flung wars against France and against our own countrymen in the American War of Independence. The most numerous lead ornaments to have survived these times were the smaller pieces such as vases, urns, jardinières and cisterns. The lead cisterns, which mostly date from the 17th and 18th centuries, and which are now collectors' items, were originally made for the purpose of collecting the rain-supply of town houses. They are nicely decorated and have now often acquired a pleasing white patina, which makes them all the more decorative for present-day courtyards (Fig. 52).

The vogue once again for statuary and urns (Plates 20 and 21) and vases in the garden came back in the 19th century when Sir Charles Barry (1795-1860), laid out a number of large formal gardens in the Italian style at Trentham Park, Staffordshire, Bowood, Wiltshire, and at Harewood House, Yorkshire. Sir Joseph Paxton at this time also favoured the Italian and highly ornamented garden and chose this style to provide a grand setting for the Crystal Palace at Sydenham. In the 1860's the most highly regarded garden designer was William Eden Nesfield who invariably adopted a rather heavy Italianate style for his layouts. This was Nesfield's inevitable choice of style for The Royal Horticultural Society's new gardens at Kensington Gore, laid out from 1862 to 1863. At Kensington Gore, as for other neo-Italian gardens, a number of sculptors were called in to provide the numerous pieces of statuary. The best figures and ornaments at this time were executed in lead, bronze, or stone, but less permanent materials were also used. As might be expected, well-known Italian Renaissance figures were the popular prototypes for sculptors commissioned to produce the decoration for these gardens. Various versions of Venus were especially favoured, as indeed had been the case throughout the 18th century, when the Goddess would be admiringly placed upon a classical column. As early as the mid-17th century a column surmounted by a bronze figure of Venus had been erected in the centre of the east forecourt at Wilton House. The actual column is of Egyptian granite and was bought by John Evelyn in Rome where it had fallen before the Temple of Venus Genetrix. The white marble base and Corinthian capital were added to the column at the time it was erected at Wilton and crowned with the statue of Venus. The column is now in a more verdant corner of the garden as a result of James Wyatt's alterations to the grounds at the beginning of the 19th century. At Chiswick House there was a column supporting a statue of Venus, but the figure has disappeared and only the column now remains.

FIG. 52. 18th-century lead cistern

However, the fashion for the Italian garden did not spread beyond the more grand schemes of gardening, despite the support given for it by Sir Reginald Blomfield in his book *The Formal Garden in England* published in 1892. Finally, William Robinson, the most influential professor of garden design at the end of the 19th century and well into the 20th century, successfully buried the idea of creating Italian gardens in this country and in its place delivered the naturalistic school of gardening. Buried also was the extravagant use of ornament, although Robinson in his *English Flower Garden* did rather begrudgingly admit that sculpture had its place in the garden, and wrote, 'A statue or two of any artistic value may be placed in a garden with good effect, never, however, forgetting that a garden is a place for beautiful life, not death.'

Although the Italian style was only applied to the more grandiose schemes of garden layout, the fashion for garden ornament in the 19th century had a more widespread following, particularly with the gardens of the rapidly growing middle classes. The supply, and no doubt some of the demand, was created by the mass-production of garden statuary and the making of substitutes for stone and marble, and the replacement of lead by cheaper metals such as iron.

The earliest substitute for stone in the production of sculptured figures and monuments was Coade ware, which was an artificial stone whose manufacture and precise composition is not known, as it was naturally a secret jealously guarded by the factory. The factory was in Belvedere Road, South Lambeth, and from about 1769 to 1837 was a most flourishing business. Mrs. Coade seems to have been an excellent head of the firm and had the foresight to engage the young sculptor John Bacon to design many of the ornaments in the early days of the enterprise. Sculptured figures of a wide variety were produced from sphinxes[1] to lions, as well as seats, urns, and monuments for the park and garden. Coade stone was also used to make elegant mouldings for buildings, church mural monuments, and table tomb monuments. Usually Coade ornaments have resisted the effects of weathering far better than natural stone. Coade ornaments are today rightly regarded as fine works of art, where the character of the material was appreciated, properly expressed and soundly designed. Coade stone is usually signed with the names of E. & W. Coade, or Coade and Seely, her partner in the latter years of the firm's existence.

FIG. 53.   18th-century stone sphinx

There were many other firms making garden ornaments in artificial stone, but the majority produced inferior work which soon disintegrated after a few years of sun and frost weathering. However, besides Coade and Seely, there were two other firms manufacturing garden ornaments in artificial stone whose ware soon gained a high reputation for quality and durability. These two firms were Cottam and Hallen, and Ransome's Siliceous Stone. Ransome's had their offices in Canon Row, Westminster, and their works at Ipswich. Their production included plinths and cornices for buildings, and for the garden they produced vases of all sizes, fountains, statues, and jardinets. The jardinet (Fig. 54) was a typical piece of Victorian decoration and was 'just the thing to face the drawing-room windows as a terrace embellishment', and was considered to be particularly suited to the Italian style of garden.

But the material that took pride of place in the 19th century was cast iron. This was the material that helped to build the Industrial Revolution and which produced some of the major engineering monuments to industrial and imperial Britain, from the early bridges and viaducts for the canals to the first great prefabricated building, the Crystal Palace of the Great Exhibition of 1851. The birthplace of the modern production of cheap cast iron and consequently the Industrial Revolution itself, was in the Midlands, and the most famous foundry there was The Coalbrook Dale Company of Shropshire. This county had all the necessary materials at hand, namely ironstone, limestone and coal, and The Coalbrook Dale Company in addition had the necessary inventiveness to produce the new methods for cheap cast iron production. The vast majority of the castings from the Midlands was of course for engineering purposes, but nevertheless the Victorian enthusiasm for cast iron led to its being used in a wide range of ornamental work, and eventually to replace most of the costly and individually produced wrought iron products. By the middle of the 19th century most ornamental ironwork was cast and not wrought, whether it was balcony railings or garden gates. In the Great Exhibition of 1851, The Coalbrook Dale Company exhibited a most comprehensive range of cast iron and

[1] Sphinxes carved in stone or cast in lead had been placed in the grounds of many famous 18th-century gardens, such as Chiswick, Bramham Park, Lacock Abbey (here one is perched on twin pillars), and at Compton Verney, and by the end of the century had become a popular form of garden ornament (Fig. 53).

24.   Stone Japanese lantern, Batsford Park, Gloucestershire

25. Children's play sculpture, Rhambshov Park,
Stockholm

FIG. 54. A Victorian jardinet, from *The National Magazine*,
1857

sometimes bronzed garden ornaments, which included ornamental park entrance gates, rustic domes (to house a central
piece of sculpture), fountains, vases with cast iron bases, ornamental flower-pots, a serpent-handled vase and base for taking
earthen flower-pots (Fig.55), rustic ornamental seats, tables,
flower stands, and boot-scrapers. Many of the designs, especially those for garden vases, were copies from classical examples
which had of course been carved in stone or marble. The great
Warwick Vase which can be seen in the orangery at Warwick
Castle, was a popular model for copying in cast iron. When they
were not simply copies from the antique they were, to our eyes at
any rate, very ornate and coarse (Fig. 56) like so many of the
consciously made 'works of art' exhibited in the 1851 Exhibition.
Looking through the three enormous volumes of the 1851

FIG. 55. Cast iron serpent-handled vase and base, made by The Coalbrook Dale Co., from the 1851 Great Exhibition catalogue

the material, and cared little for imitations from other ages. The lesson here is that the Victorians separated art from industry and science, and consequently gave rise to the dead-end cult of art for art's sake. This unfortunate cleavage of art and science and technology along with the art-for-art's-sake mentality still remains with us today, and is too often apparent in our popular attitude to garden and landscape design. It results in the belief that is sometimes held that the artist should only be employed on the design of non-functional objects in a landscape or townscape, that a fountain is a work of art (although originally it was also a functional object), but that the aesthetic qualities of modern functional features such as lighting columns and similar pieces of street furniture need not be considered. A more rational approach would be to see that the modern man-made objects should be well designed and good-looking, just as our mediaeval forefathers made the market place fountain an aesthetically pleasing feature, as well as a functional one. Likewise, water can provide other delights besides visual ones, in particular for children to paddle and splash in.

catalogue today, one is more likely to be charmed by the exhibits that were not thought to be artistic at the time, such as the fine engravings of machinery, bridges and other engineering works where the designers were more sensitive to the true character of

FIG. 56. Bronzed cast iron vase by Andrew Handyside, Britannia Foundry, Derby, from the 1851 Great Exhibition catalogue

FIGS. 57-58. The Britannia vase and Tazza vase, from Messrs. Boulton and Paul's catalogue of 1896

However, the 1851 Exhibition was at the peak of high Victorian design, for by the end of the century the design of garden ornaments was much more refined, and those later examples are consequently more sought after as decoration for today's gardens. Messrs. Boulton and Paul's catalogue of 1896[1] gives an interesting range of vases, fencing, arches, bowers, and a fountain in cast and wrought iron, which are all of a pleasing design and are well

[1] Messrs. Boulton and Paul no longer manufacture garden ornament.

proportioned with none of the early excesses in decoration. The prices for these cast iron vases were 8s. 9d. for the 'Tazza', and the pedestal 6s. 6d. extra, 10s. 6d. for the 'Britannia' (Fig. 57), and the larger 'Tazza' vase (Fig. 58) was 17s. 6d. and 21s. extra for the

FIG. 59.   Wrought iron plant vase, Rous Lench, Worcestershire

pedestal.   Many of these vases can be seen today in gardens and parks throughout the country, and of course, in dealers' yards. Boulton and Paul's catalogue of 1896 also listed an attractive wrought iron garden vase made up of iron straps and hoops. This was priced at 13s. for an eighteen-inch-diameter vase, and 26s. 6d. for a thirty-six-inch-diameter one.   Many of these attractive vases still exist in gardens, usually in good condition as is the one illustrated in Fig. 59, at Rous Lench, Worcestershire.   It was designed to be filled in the way a hanging-basket is stocked each year with the outside of the filling composed of moss to retain the inner core of soil and plants.

Wirework was also used to make vases and flower-baskets. Fewer of these have survived, and only those that have been regularly painted, and this was more often confined to the charming wire flower-tables and seats.   The popularity of the wire flower-basket came in with the reintroduction of flower gardening in the early 19th century.   Humphry Repton was responsible for this break with the landscape school of gardening of the 18th century when in his later years he divided the garden up into a number of specialised parts.   At Ashridge Park, Hertfordshire, in about 1812 Repton provided gardens that were separated from the landscape park.   These separate gardens included an American garden, a parterre, a Rosarium, a monk's garden, a Cabinet de Verdure, and so on.   Several of these gardens or proposals for

gardens by the mature Repton, made much use of flowers and even had flower-beds and flower-baskets in the lawn.   Repton's

FIG. 60.   Wire flower-basket for the garden.

FIG. 61. Wire hanging flower-basket

Both from Mrs. Loudon's *Ladies' Companion to the Flower Garden,* 1841

proposals for the gardens of the Royal Pavilion at Brighton had flowers in the lawn, tidily kept in place by wire baskets or wire edging.   The flower garden around the house soon became the special interest for the ladies of the house.   Mrs. Loudon in her famous book *Ladies' Companion to the Flower Garden,* published in 1841, recommends the use of wire flower-baskets in the garden. They could be raised on pedestals or fixed on the ground (Fig. 60). The latter are 'furnished with sharp spikes for entering the ground, like the prongs of a fork; and these are placed so as to form a circle with wires for climbing plants extended across it, like the handles of a basket.   The plants must be trained up a wire frame in the centre, and thence brought down the wires to the curved pieces of iron forming the border of the basket,' wrote Mrs. Loudon.   She also went on to describe two hanging-baskets for the garden or conservatory, which had been adopted by a Captain Mangles, 'whose taste in ornamental gardening is well known'.   One of these baskets was called the 'China Flower-Basket' (Fig. 62) and was made from wickerwork, whilst the other (Fig. 61) was made of wire.   Wire stands were also popular at about this time, and as these were painted, many have survived as garden ornaments to this day.   They were usually made up of several tiers, rather like a wedding cake (Fig. 63), and are usually most elegant stands for the conservatory or verandah.   Mrs. Loudon says that they were generally painted green, which would seem a poor choice of colour, as it would almost certainly clash with the foliage of the plants, and would not show the intricate pattern of the wirework as well as white paint.   Mrs. Loudon gives useful and practical advice on the planting of flower-stands when she advises that all the plants should be in double pots, or

26. Children's play sculpture, Rhambshov Park, Stockholm

that the interstices of the stand should be filled with moss in order to reduce the drying effects of wind and sun. Today we have non-porous pots that would also help to reduce the loss of moisture from plants grown in this way.

Mrs. Loudon's husband, John Claudius, the foremost writer on gardening and a leading landscape gardener of the day, also recommended baskets and 'props' for the flower garden, and in his *Encyclopaedia of Gardening* went so far as to suggest that 'even the apiary, and aviary, or, at least here and there a beehive, or a cage suspended from a tree, will form very appropriate ornaments. Sometimes inoffensive birds, as the sea-gull, may be introduced to run at large; gold-fish are very appropriate in the aquarium; and an animal which affords great amusement by its cry and song in the flower gardens of the south of Germany, the tree frog (*Rana*

arborea), would be an acquisition in this country.' The more general provision and interest in local wild birds in the garden is a comparatively recent concern. In this century it has been recognised that although birds can do much damage to early flowers and buds, and to fruit generally, they also do much good in the garden by keeping down the numbers of our many insect pests. In addition an astonishingly large following has grown up in this century for bird-watching. In the 1920's and '30's stone or lead bird-baths were one of the most common garden ornaments to be manufactured. Many of these bird-baths were, unfortunately, poorly designed and equally badly executed, particularly some of the designs made in cast stone. But more expensive ones carved in stone were of better standard, both in design and execution, and many of the lead bird-baths have all

FIG. 64.   Lead bird bath

FIG. 62.   Wickerwork
hanging flower-basket

FIG. 63   Wire flower-
stand

Both from Mrs. Loudon's *Ladies' Companion to the Flower
Garden*, 1841

the traditional charm of good garden ornamental leadwork. A few firms still specialise in the manufacture of lead bird-baths. The usual pattern has a circular bath with decorated sides, and often with a life-size bird cast on to the rim (Fig. 64). Besides the ornamental value of the bird-bath it also provides a place in hot weather where the birds can bathe and in freezing conditions a vital supply of water, providing the bath is frequently filled with warm water. In this way the bird-bath will attract a large number and a wide variety of wild birds to the private garden, the school courtyard, factory garden or public park, and so give to our ever-increasing urban population much innocent pleasure and delight.

In some Edwardian gardens there was a minor vogue for sculptured figures of animals, modelled in a very naturalistic style. These ornaments were usually cast in lead, bronze, or gun metal, and were placed in the wilder parts of the garden, as in the case of the well-modelled lead figures of deer at Batsford Park, Gloucestershire (Plate 22). Figures of lions were also manufactured as garden ornaments and were popularly placed in the wild garden or at the end of an Edwardian garden vista.

During the Edwardian period the grounds attached to large country houses were composed of a number of separate and specialised gardens, such as wild gardens, woodland gardens, water and bog gardens, alpine and rock gardens, rose gardens, and sometimes Japanese gardens. The Japanese gardens in 20th-

century Britain naturally contained appropriate ornaments and in particular the stone lantern.

In Japan the stone or bronze lantern was originally designed for presenting votive offerings in the gardens and courts of Buddhist temples and shrines. The Japanese gardeners went to considerable trouble to site correctly the lanterns in the garden where they formed a stylised composition with rocks, shrubs, pine trees, and water. Today the Japanese rarely have a light in the fire box or head of the lantern, but instead look upon the lantern purely as an ornament in the garden. There are two main classes of Japanese lanterns, the standard type, sometimes known as a Kasuga lantern—after a Shinto god—(Plate 24) and the legged type or Snow Scene lantern, which stands on two or more legs and has an umbrella-shaped roof. The latter feature makes a good collecting surface for snow which to the Japanese makes an as beautiful effect in the garden as do flowers.

As the Japanese garden became more popular in Britain, especially for small gardens and public parks, so the quality of the ornaments deteriorated, and soon badly made and poorly designed copies of Japanese lanterns were manufactured and put on the popular market.

One of the biggest changes that has taken place in our national mode of living during this century has been the growth of suburbs. The gardens in these suburban housing estates are primarily used as pleasure grounds, where gardening has often become an absorbing hobby and a means of self-expression. Much of the decoration and ornament made for these gardens is a part of the popular art of our times. Gnomes and dwarfs; concrete toadstools painted with white spots on a lurid red background; shoddy and ridiculously out-of-scale imitation well-heads, and concrete staddle-stones have been manufactured by the thousand, and used to make countless front gardens ridiculous. The essential ingredient of these ornaments is sentiment—everything else is sacrificed to this notion. To this end they must therefore imitate something familiar from the past, no matter how useless this object may now be or how unsympathetic this may be to the modern material that is being used. The best one can say is that garden ornament for the suburban garden is still a young art, insufficiently aware of good past traditions, but with a world to win in the way of improved standards.

The best of today's sculptured ornament for the garden comes from individual commissions to sculptors. The cost of such work is naturally high, particularly when it is carved in stone or cast in metal. However, new techniques, such as those concerning the use of *ciment-fondu*, can greatly reduce the cost (Plate 23). Furthermore, if quality can only be preferred to quantity, it will surely be found that one really well designed and executed piece of sculpture will be much more admired and give more pleasure over a longer period than any number of mass-produced dwarfs and gnomes.

Sculpture in the garden or park is most successful when it is in scale with its surroundings. Life-size sculpture of the human figure is perhaps the most difficult to provide with a setting that is properly in scale. Larger-than-life-size figures have a monumental character that is above competition from life and will always stand successfully on its own. Truly monumental works are best sited in exposed positions, to close vistas, or where sculpture has to compete with large trees, expansive lawns, or extensive views. The small-scale figure is most easily and successfully sited in the unexpected corners of a garden, where the setting is small and intimate, and where sculpture will add greater meaning to the place.

Sculpture for gardens, public parks, town squares and playgrounds has nowhere been better used and more sympathetically designed for the open-air setting than in Scandinavia. In those countries sculpture has been used to enhance and provide a focal point for the many delightful landscapes associated with the new buildings and recreational areas. It has been designed as play-sculpture for children (Plates 25 and 26) and combined with utilitarian objects such as drinking fountains, and gives a great deal of delight to children and adults alike.

Sculpture can also be applied in a variety of ways to garden walls. Carving brickwork, so as to make a design in relief, is a most effective decoration, or alternatively, materials can be applied to the wall. In both cases the decoration is made more telling by the strong contrast of light and shade, so that north walls are best avoided. The International Gardens Exhibition at Hamburg in 1963 used for screening purposes a number of white-painted walls, some of which had a most lively and cheap form of mural decoration from wires fixed a few inches from the surface of the wall. When there was strong light, and particularly with full sunshine or artificial lighting at night, the tracery of the wires cast a strong pattern on to the surface of the wall. Similar mural decoration could be most striking if used in courtyards or patio gardens.

Sculpture when in close association with plants is most likely to be successful if it provides a contrast with the intricacy and detail of vegetation. Large smooth surfaces, particularly of stone, will provide good contrast. Indeed pleasingly shaped boulders or well-weathered rocks provide a focal point in a corner of a landscape and will give the necessary contrast to the plants. Success will depend on the selection of the rocks or boulders and their satisfactory arrangement. With well-weathered rocks or water-worn boulders there is a quality of permanence and ageless beauty. Weathering of the rock surface and the growth of lichen and mosses gives the rock a harmonious but fascinating range of colours and surfaces. The Japanese have developed a great love and appreciation for rocks and boulders, and have used them in their gardens with great skill. It is not uncommon in Japan for nurserymen to have for sale rocks and boulders that have been selected from the mountainside because of their sculptural value in the garden. To use rocks successfully in a sculptural way in the garden it is essential to appreciate their beauty of shape and form and not use them simply to provide a home for rock plants, or to imitate slavishly a mountain outcrop.

Chapter Four

TOPIARY

TOPIARY is defined by the dictionary as the art of clipping and growing trees and shrubs into ornamental shapes. This definition covers the well-known topiary figures, knot gardens, some types of parterres, and garden mazes, when these are made from vegetation.

To be most effective, topiary should be practised on slow-growing, but long-living evergreen trees and shrubs. Obviously the smaller the leaf the plant possesses, the less it will show the marks of clipping. The most common plants to be treated as topiary subjects are yew, box, cypress, poet's laurel or sweet bay, holly, privet, juniper, beech, hornbeam, and rosemary.

Some form of topiary seems to have come naturally to the repertoire of the ornamental gardener during most civilisations, usually at a time when the landscape outside the cultivated areas about the settlements was less controlled and orderly than it is today. In Europe topiary has been used as the major feature of some great gardens, as well as being the single centre-piece of some humble but nonetheless charming English cottage gardens. Some European nations have favoured topiary more than others. The Dutch for several centuries were the masters of the art and craft of 'verdant sculpture' and the idea of a Dutch garden in Britain is usually associated with some form of topiary work. The French have remained most loyal to the following of topiary work, finding in this extreme form of art dominating nature a sense of urbanity and sophistication. Topiary in France has never had the violent opposition to it that occurred in England during the early part of the 18th century. The French have even extended a form of topiary to the kitchen garden with their superbly trained fruit trees in the form of goblets, animals and letters of the alphabet, and in the animal kingdom to their favourite dog, the poodle. As an art topiary is more truly a folk art than a fine art. Few, if any, professional artists have been concerned with the design of individual topiary figures.

All the early pleasure gardens in Europe were not only formal in design and therefore in strict contrast with the wild outside world, but were also places where the vegetation had to be disciplined into artificial shapes. Shrubs often would be chastised by the topiarists; plant beds would be laid out as knots of intertwining and clipped herbs; hedges made formal by clipping and the enclosing alleys of trees would be pleached. The knot garden became popular in England early in the 15th century. The plants selected for this type of garden were mostly aromatic herbs such as basil, fennel, lavender, hysop, marjoram, sage, and mints. The clippings from the aromatic herbs provided welcome material for strewing on to the rush floors of the none too sanitary Tudor houses of the time. In this way the pungent herbs

27. Topiary chessmen, Compton
Wynyates, Warwickshire

would suppress some of the undesirable domestic Tudor airs! More elaborate and larger forms of the knot garden were invented with the parterre gardens in 16th-century France. Some of these parterres were mainly composed of shrubs clipped to scrolls and invariably flat on top. The gardens at Villandry in the Loire valley, France, contain some of the finest gardens of this type existing today. Nearly all the gardens contain low flat box hedges, laid out in formal shapes. The *Jardin d'Amour* for instance is made up of numerous box beds in the shapes of hearts and daggers, which in the summer are now filled with colourful flowering plants. Even the *Jardin Potager* has been laid out in a geometric design, with the numerous beds enclosed by box hedges. Topiary pyramids or cones might be introduced to emphasise certain points in the design. In the 19th century Villandry was affected by the English landscape movement, for the old formal gardens were destroyed to make way for a *parc anglais*. However, early in the 20th century the owners restored these unique gardens to something like their former appearance by replanning them to a design by the famous French 16th-century garden maker, Du Cerceau.

Whilst it is sometimes claimed that the Egyptians had topiary in their gardens, it is the Roman writers who have given us the first recorded description of topiary work. Some of these descriptions of Roman topiary show that many of their gardens had a most extravagant display of 'verdant sculpture'. Descriptions are given of fleets of ships or a complete hunting scene carried out in topiary work. After the fall of Rome, when the Empire became centred on Constantinople, the style of gardening reached a most fantastic stage, with true topiary replaced by exotically jewelled trees, which were often further decorated with colourful birds. From Byzantium the arts of gardening were gradually spread throughout Europe mainly thanks at first to the Crusaders, but later by various monastic orders. Mediaeval monastic gardens throughout Europe favoured topiary as a means of providing both seclusion and embellishment. From the monastery to the manor house topiary continued to be an important feature of the pleasure garden. Most of the mediaeval topiary was, however, very simple, just small trees cut into geometric shapes or into tiers. The more elaborate figures were produced in the 16th and 17th centuries.

The 16th century saw the start of the golden age of topiary, which in England continued until the beginning of the 18th century. The Dutch were the masters of topiary work, and when the Dutch garden became popular in Britain during the reign of William and Mary, topiary became an important part of orna-mental gardening in this country. The leading garden designers in England about this time were George London and Henry Wise, who appear to have always employed a great deal of topiary in their designs. They were the authors of an abridged and 'improved' edition of John Evelyn's *Compleat Gardener* which Evelyn had earlier translated from the French. London and Wise had the then well-known nursery at Brompton to supply them and others with the fashionable plants of the day. Following the new building work by Christopher Wren at Hampton Court, Wise was commissioned to alter and enlarge the gardens in the French style. He laid out the large semi-circular garden, which originally contained a great deal of topiary. Chatsworth and Melbourne Hall, those two magnificent Derbyshire homes, were also further commissions for London and Wise. The gardens at Melbourne Hall remain little altered today, and are a fine testimony to their abilities as garden designers working in the grand formal manner. By the end of the 17th century topiary had become something of a national craze, just as carpet-bedding was to so obsess the gardeners of the mid-Victorian era.

This craze for the extravagant use of topiary inevitably produced a reaction which swung the pendulum of taste so violently in the opposite direction that most formal gardens and topiary work were swept away in the new naturalistic style of gardening that developed in England in the 18th century. Few great topiary gardens survived the sudden change in fashion. The notable exceptions were the gardens at Levens Hall, Westmorland, which were laid out in 1701-4 by Beaumont, the French garden designer working in England at that time; some of the topiary at Rous Lench, Worcestershire; and the famous yew garden at Packwood, Warwickshire, which represents the Sermon on the Mount and the Multitude. The topiary gardens at Levens Hall today present a most extraordinary Alice-in-Wonderland world of yew and box, trees shaped in the forms of birds, animals, crowns, tables, jugs, chairs, chessmen, bottles, spirals, and cones. Other examples survived in the front gardens of a number of English cottages whose style of gardening remained vernacular and therefore impervious to the whims of fashionable taste. Many of the large umbrageous yews that we see in older gardens today were no doubt originally trained into the shapes of dragons, men, pyramids or columns, but have since been allowed to lose their representational shapes. The large yews in the great semi-circular garden at Hampton Court, for example, were in their more youthful days trim pyramids.

William Lawson in his book *A New Orchard and Garden*, published in 1618, wrote that 'your gardener can frame your lesser

28. Topiary figure of a Beefeater,
Compton Wynyates, Warwickshire

wood to the shape of men armed in the field, ready to give battell; or swift running greyhounds; or of well scented and true running Hounds to chase the Deere, or hunt the Hare. This kind of hunting shall not waste your corne, nor much your coyne!' However, from what Francis Bacon (1561-1626) wrote in his essay *Of Gardens* it would appear that not everyone even at this time was completely taken with the craze for topiary. 'As for the making of knots, or figures, with divers coloured earths, that they may lie under the windows of the house, on that side which the garden stands, they be but toys: you may see as good sights many times in tarts' Bacon scornfully declared. A little farther on in the essay he wrote 'I for my part, do not like images cut out in juniper or other garden stuff; they be for children.'

By the early 18th century the excesses and absurdities of formalism together with the ubiquitous use of the shears brought such leading literary figures as Joseph Addison and then Alexander Pope to ridicule the current taste in gardening. Addison in the *Spectator* in 1712 in his essay *On the Pleasures of the Imagination* wrote 'we have observed something more grand and august than what we meet with in the curiosities of art . . .' and complains that 'our British gardeners instead of humouring nature, love to deviate from it as much as possible. Our trees rise in cones, globes, and pyramids. We see the marks of the scissors upon every plant and bush. I do not know whether I am singular in my opinion, but for my own part, I would rather look upon a tree in all its luxuriancy and diffusion of boughs and branches, than

29.   Topiary figure of a cat, Compton Wynyates, Warwickshire

when it is thus cut and trimmed into a mathematical figure, and cannot but fancy that an orchard in flower looks infinitely more delightful than all the little labyrinths of the most finished parterre.' A little later in the same year Addison invents a correspondent who describes an imaginary garden laid out with 'the beautiful wildness of nature, without effecting the nicer elegancies of art'.

A year after Addison's attack on topiary, *The Guardian* on the 29th September, 1713, published Alexander Pope's famous satirical essay on 'verdant sculpture'. 'I believe it is no wrong observation,' wrote Pope 'that persons of Genius, and those who are most capable of Art, are always most fond of Nature, as such are chiefly sensible, that all Art consists in the Imitation and Study of Nature. On the contrary, People of the common Level of Understanding are principally delighted with the little Niceties and Fantastical Operations of Art, and constantly think that finest which is least Natural. A Citizen is no sooner Proprietor of a Couple of Yews, but he entertains Thoughts of erecting them into Giants, like those of Guildhall. I know an eminent Cook, who beautified his Country Seat with a Coronation Dinner in Greens, where you see the Champion flourishing on Horseback at one end of the Table, and the Queen in perpetual Youth at the other.'

Pope finishes his essay with a 'Catalogue of Greens to be disposed of by an eminent Town-Gardener . . .

'Adam and Eve in Yew; Adam a little shatter'd by the fall of the Tree of Knowledge in the great Storm: Eve and the Serpent very flourishing.

'The Tower of Babel, not yet finished.

'St. George in Box; his Arm scarce long enough, but will be in a Condition to stick the Dragon by next April.

'A green Dragon of the same, with a Tail of Ground Ivy for the present.

'N.B. These two not to be Sold separately.

'Edward the Black Prince in Cypress.

'A Laurustine Bear in Blossom, with a Juniper Hunter in Berries.

'A Pair of Giants, stunted, to be sold cheap.

'A Queen Elisabeth in Phylyraea, a little inclining to the Green Sickness, but of full Growth.

'Another Queen Elisabeth in Myrtle, which was very forward, but miscarried by being too near a Savine.

'An old Maid of Honour in Wormwood.

'A topping Ben Jonson in Laurel.

'Divers eminent modern Poets in Bays, somewhat blighted, to be disposed of, a Pennyworth.

'A Quick-set Hog shot up into a Porcupine, by its being forgot a Week in rainy Weather.

'A Lavender Pig with Sage growing in his Belly.

'Noah's Ark in Holly, standing on the Mount; the Ribs a little damaged for want of Water.

'A Pair of Maidenheads in Fir, in great forwardness.'

Bacon and now Addison and Pope, the reputed leaders of taste from the literary world, had attacked the contemporary vogue for topiary in English gardens. Pope was the most successful attacker and ridicule the most telling weapon. The topiarists soon fled from the scene and their gardens suffered large casualties which were quickly buried beneath the more chaste lawns of the picturesque gardens. William Kent, and later Capability Brown and Humphry Repton, the professional leaders of the picturesque landscape style, not only occupied the positions formerly held by London and Wise, the exponents of the topiary garden, but consolidated and developed gardening to a leading and influential position in the environmental arts in England. In a remarkably few years after Pope's essay in *The Guardian* Horace Walpole, as always, was able to sum up the position in his usual masterly manner 'Improvements had gone till London and Wise had stocked our gardens with giants, animals, monsters, coats-of-arms and mottoes in yew, box and holly. Absurdities could go no further, and the tide turned.'

Most of the examples of topiary, knot, and parterre gardens that we see today date from the revival of this style of gardening that occurred in the mid-19th century. The architectural or Italianate gardens laid out by Sir Charles Barry (1795-1860), and Eden Nesfield contained parterre gardens with evergreens planted and trimmed to form scrolls and volutes within a strictly formal layout. Although the Italian garden became far less popular by the end of the 19th century, some topiary work continued to form a part of most large garden layouts. The Victorians felt that topiary gave an old-world charm to the otherwise all too new and immature grounds of the many recently built country estates. Two of the famous topiary gardens built in the 19th century were at Elvaston Castle, Derbyshire, and at Compton Wynyates, Warwickshire: surprisingly the latter garden was planted as late as 1895 (Plates 27, 28, and 29). Even more recently planted topiary, but again looking fully mature, is in the National Trust gardens at Hidcote, Gloucestershire, and Nymans in Sussex.

During the early part of this century a number of nurseries in this country made a speciality of topiary growing. Messrs. Cheal and Sons of Crawley, Sussex, and Messrs. William Cutbush and Son of Highgate, London, were well known topiary suppliers at this time.   William Cutbush imported many of his fine specimens from the old masters of topiary, the Dutch, as well as growing and training many thousands of topiary subjects in his nursery.

To create and maintain a topiary garden successfully, an open and sunny site should be selected which also has or can be given protection from severe winds.   The soil should preferably be loam, or at least have good-quality loam incorporated into the topsoil.   Inorganic manures should be avoided.   Well-rotted farmyard manure or compost, coarse bonemeal and liquid manure are the best forms of feeding for evergreen trees such as yew and box, the commonest plants of topiary treatment.   Planting is best carried out in early autumn or in the spring.   Tub-grown specimens can, of course, be planted at most times of the year when the ground is free from frost.   Evergreen trees and shrubs should be moved with as large a root-ball of soil as is necessary to contain most of the roots.   Mulching around the roots should continue for several years after planting, and again in later years if the trees appear to have exhausted the soil of available plant nutrients.   This exhaustion of the surrounding soil is most likely to occur on light sandy formations.   Clipping should be carried out in August and the early part of September.   For the mature specimens it will usually be necessary to clip within one and a half to two inches of the previous year's growth in order to keep the trees within reasonable bounds.   Heavy falls of snow can be most damaging to some specimens of topiary, when ledges and branches are bent down and misshapen or broken by the weight of snow.   Early removal of heavy clinging snow can, of course, avoid this unfortunate destruction of years of patient training.

Mazes or labyrinths are usually associated with topiary, as most of the well-known mazes in this country are garden ones formed from hedges such as yew, box, beech, and privet.

A maze or labyrinth consists of a number of enclosed paths or passages which are laid out in such a way that the visitor to the maze repeatedly loses his way attempting to get to the centre of the maze or in simply trying to get out again.

The labyrinth is a term usually applied to unenclosed paths that eventually lead one to the designed end, whereas the maze is formed from enclosed or partly enclosed walks whose design has a number of blocked ends or culs-de-sac.   Early labyrinths were laid out with inlaid marble slabs in the floors of cathedrals and churches on the Continent.   It is thought that penitents had to follow the path of the labyrinth on their hands and knees, offering prayers on the slow and laborious route.

The origin of mazes goes back into antiquity and many reasons have been put forward by historians for their early construction. The Greeks attached importance to the medical value of mazes,

30.   Children's log maze, Birmingham Parks Department

particularly for helping to improve the patients' mental attitude towards medical treatment. It was reasoned that in the maze the patient would undergo a symbolical break with his set attitude or pattern of thought and could then later be purged of his troubles.

The earliest mazes in Britain were simply cut in the turf, and were made up of a number of paths surrounded on either side by turf banks. A number of these turf mazes still survive, notably the one on St. Catherine's Hill, near Winchester, at Wing, Rutlandshire, and at Skensby, Yorkshire. It is thought that they were originally constructed for races or games on horseback. The game was called City of Troy. The Romans practised a similar game called Troy Game. The game consisted of intricate movements for the horse and its rider which were designed to improve or exhibit the rider's powers of horsemanship. It is interesting to find that a number of similar turf mazes also survive in Scandinavia and were presumably used for similar purposes as they are called Trojeborg (Troy Town).

Garden mazes as a garden feature obviously have a number of attractions for they offer a certain amount of adventure or fascination in walking into the unknown, as well as providing privacy and amusement in the garden. The maze became a popular feature in gardens in Britain, along with other forms of topiary, in the 17th century. The most famous garden maze surviving from this period is the one planted in yew at Hampton Court in the late 17th century, when new gardens were laid out to the designs of Christopher Wren and the gardener Henry Wise.

Hedged garden mazes were planted in several 19th-century gardens, such as the one at Woburn Park, Bedfordshire, the pagoda at the centre of which is shown in Plate 7, and occasionally for children with low hedging as can be seen at Wootton Court, Warwickshire. As play places for children they can be most popular and provide endless amusement. The City of Birmingham Parks Department have recently constructed some children's mazes with larch logs (Plate 30) which have proved more popular than many more sophisticated and expensive playthings.

Chapter Five

WATER ORNAMENTS

================== ⟜⟞⟞⟝⟝ ==================

*Spring-, well-, and conduit-heads; joke fountains; fountains and
basons; cascades; cold baths; Sir Joseph Paxton's use of fountains;
Victorian fountains; Sir Edwin Lutyens's water gardens; wall
fountain masks; fountains and paddling pools; lead cisterns;
Italian well-heads; water pumps; Victorian drinking fountains.*

THE natural supply of fresh water played a vital part in the choice of early human settlement. Away from rivers and lakes the supply of water for drinking and washing came from springs or wells. The importance of such wells or springs to a community led to their development as meeting-places for social gossip and trading, and naturally led to their elaboration and embellishment. Scenes depicted on ancient Egyptian and Greek vases, for instance, often show decorated well-heads. With the building in mediaeval times of self-supporting establishments such as monasteries and manor houses, the well or spring was made into an important feature of the ornamental grounds. In the market place and in the gardens during mediaeval times the well-head and the conduit-head were often developed into a most elaborate and decorated feature. The overflow pipes from a conduit- or spring-head were made into fountains, often in the form of animal head masks, which would spout water into a basin from which it would flow through channels to form pools at lower levels, and finally to leave the garden via a culvert constructed under the boundary wall.

The fountain and well-head remained the most important and elaborate feature in the garden throughout mediaeval times and up to the early Renaissance period. The most famous early Renaissance conduit-head in England is at Trinity College, Cambridge, and dates from 1602. It stands in the middle of the Great Court, and makes one of the most impressive centre-pieces in Cambridge.

In the Renaissance villa garden in Italy, water was one of the most important elements in the layout, and the art and science of fountain construction reached perfection. Whole rivers were diverted to feed the many water features in the garden, and engineers such as Olivieri specialised in their design.

In France the Renaissance garden of the 17th century continued to use—often in a most lavish way—fountains and other water ornaments. Trick or joke fountains were also developed and although they were more common on the Continent, we have a number of contemporary descriptions of similar fountains built in gardens in England.

The purpose of the joke fountain was to give the innocent visitor to the garden a soaking as a reward for curiosity. The now vanished gardens of Nonsuch Palace, Surrey, originally contained one of the earliest examples in this country of trick fountains. The building of Nonsuch Palace as a hunting lodge for King Henry VIII was begun in 1538 and its gardens soon became among the most celebrated in England. Through the patronage of Henry VIII a number of artists and craftsmen were induced to come to England from the Continent, and so encourage the quicker growth of Renaissance culture in the kingdom. John of Padua, an architect who designed in a very disciplined Classical style, was a leading figure in the introduction of Renaissance architecture into Britain. The garden ornament for Nonsuch Palace was almost certainly the work of Italian artists and craftsmen, and the knowledge required to construct such elaborate waterworks would have then had to come from the Continent. The Privy Garden at Nonsuch contained several fountains, many of marble, placed at the intersections of the paths. The Venus fountain was one of the grandest, even if a little hearty, for water spouted from the breasts of the goddess. The trick waterworks were in the form of a marble pyramid which concealed a number of pipes that could spout water on unsuspecting visitors.

The Renaissance garden for Wilton House, Wiltshire, laid out by Isaac de Caus or Caux[1] in 1632, contained a great many fountains including some trick ones. The fountains here were almost certainly inspired or derived from continental designs, in common with most garden ornament at that time. In the grotto at Wilton there were, for instance, 'many fine figures of ye Goddesses, and about 2 yards off the doore is several pipes in a line that with a sluce spouths water up to wett the strangers'. Celia Fiennes gives an account of these joke fountains and mentions that they were in a chamber from the main grotto from which 'the water runs in the rocks . . . and makes the melody of Nightingerls which engages the curiosity of strangers to go in to see, but at the entrance of each room is a line of pipes that appear not till moved by a sluce it washes the spectator for a diversion'. De Caus' trick waterworks remained for many years one of the most celebrated features of the gardens at Wilton, until the grounds were transformed in the 18th and 19th centuries.

Other trick fountains were at that time to be found at Hampton Court, Whitehall, London, and Chatsworth, Derbyshire. At Chatsworth there is still a willow tree fountain standing in Paxton's rock garden. The present one was made in 1829 and is thought to have been an exact reproduction of the original one made by the smith Ibeck in 1693. The fountain is a trick one and consists of a weeping tree built in metal that can be made to weep a generous flow of water down on to unsuspecting visitors.

[1] Isaac de Caus was a Frenchman and came to England to take over from a relative the work of laying out gardens in England in the French Renaissance style.

To make this joke even more of 'a diversion' numerous jets were hidden in the surrounding rocks which could be operated on instructions from the Duke, by a gardener hiding behind a peephole wall!

To derive amusement continually from joke fountains, such as the willow tree fountain at Chatsworth, something of the custard-pie type of humour is required. The Russians seem particularly to enjoy this brand of humour. Many of their public parks in Leningrad and in Moscow have joke fountains of the willow tree type that occasionally soak visitors, including statesmen from Western countries!

Francis Bacon (1561-1626), in his famous essay *Of Gardens* made no reference to such amusements as trick fountains for the garden. Instead he praised the purely ornamental fountains and stressed the disadvantages of stagnant pools. 'For fountains,' wrote Bacon, 'they are a great beauty and refreshment; but pools mar all, and make the garden unwholesome and full of flies and frogs.' He went on to mention that the fountains made in 'images gilt, or marble, which are in use, do well; but the main matter is, so to convey the water as it never stay, either in the bowls or in the cistern, that the water be never by rest discoloured, green or red, or the like, or gather any mossiness or putrefaction. Besides that,

31. Cold bath, Packwood House, Warwickshire

it is cleansed every day by hand.' Sound practical advice for fountains in gardens which unfortunately is all too often ignored. Fountains in Bacon's day were made to form with jets a variety of elaborate shapes. In his essay *Of Gardens* he mentions fountains forming the shapes of feathers, drinking glasses, and canopies, whilst other writers described jets forming crowns, birds and animals.

Other than at Chatsworth and Melbourne Hall, Derbyshire, few of these 17th-century waterworks are in existence today, except as formal canals and *basons* robbed of the fountains they once contained. The *basons* in which many of the fountains played were then an essential part of a garden in the French style. *Basons* would be built near the house to be looked down on from the important rooms, and to provide reflections of the sky by day and perhaps fireworks by night. The water of the *basons* also reflected light on to the façade of the house and so enlivened the architectural details of the building, in the same way, although less strongly, as the stone-flagged terrace will flatteringly reflect light up to the face of a building. The *basons* were always of a formal shape, varying from circular to oblong, with classical moulding for the walls. The depth of a *bason* rarely exceeded two feet, which together with its stone floor, would facilitate easy and regular cleaning. Examples of these Renaissance *basons* in England can be seen at Chatsworth, Bramham Park, Yorkshire, Melbourne Hall, Derbyshire, Wrest Park, Bedfordshire, Studley Royal, Yorkshire, and at Hampton Court. The sea-horse fountain and *bason* carved by Caius Gabriel Cibber, in the late 17th century, still remains today in the gardens at Chatsworth. Most of the other *basons* in this country were completely removed in the 18th century, as they were considered far too artificial and unnatural in the pastoral setting that most owners then strove to create.

Great stone cascades constructed down a garden hillside are mostly associated with Renaissance villa gardens of Italy. But at Chatsworth a noble cascade, on the Italian grand scale, was built down the hillside at the back of the house, and has been retained as a major feature in the garden despite the changing whims of fashion. It was designed by the Frenchman Grillet and completed in 1696, but since that date it has been enlarged and given a Cascade House designed by Thomas Archer.

During the picturesque or natural landscape period of gardening that lasted throughout most of the 18th century and into the 19th century, fountains and other obviously artificial water features were rarely constructed in Britain. Man-made waters were designed to look like rivers or lakes, and a cascade, instead of being an architectural *tour-de-force*, now resembled a natural fall of water as might be seen in wild nature. William Kent particularly liked to have a rock-strewn cascade at one end of his natural-looking designed waters. A typical cascade by Kent (built in the late 1730's) can be seen today at Chiswick House at one end of the artificial 'River Ches'. Unfortunately the cascade is no longer supplied with a good flow of water, as was originally intended. The Hon. Charles Hamilton, one of the early pioneers of natural landscaping, derived his inspiration for the naturalistic cascade he built for his friend the Marquis of Lansdowne at Bowood, Wiltshire, from a much admired landscape painting by Gaspar Poussin. No longer were English gardens being laid out on French or Italian lines, instead they now followed the landscape painter's eye, and the poet's imagination as so well expressed by Alexander Pope:

> Consult the Genius of the Place in all;
> That tells the Waters or to rise, or fall;

Basons and canals were now 'improved' and made to look like natural lakes or rivers, and new waters were laid out to resemble natural stretches of water. To begin with the scale of these waters was modest, but by Capability Brown's time, the damming of streams to create large lakes was a normal part of the landscaping of country estates. The water features of William Kent's design for the new gardens at Rousham, Oxfordshire, were, for example, quite small in size. The formal outline of the two existing ponds was made irregular and naturalistic but little enlarged, and the water supply to and from the cold bath was made to run in a curving and a most charming little stone rill. Surprisingly, at Rousham, the cold bath remained straightforward and formal in design. At this early stage of the landscape movement, not all formalism was swept aside, and certainly not for this largely functional garden amenity.

The cold bath throughout the 17th and 18th centuries was a fairly common provision in the garden. It was primarily used by men hot from hunting or other athletic pursuits, or during exceptional summer weather, when a plunge into chilly water would be welcome. The bathers must have been very warm-blooded indeed, for the baths were invariably sited in shady places, and were fed from chilly water, often from a spring. At Rousham there is a stone building beside the bath that was used as a changing room. Sometimes the changing room would be well equipped, and have a chimney and fireplace for reviving numbed bodies! Occasionally the bath was completely roofed over or constructed in the grotto. They were always attractively built, with fine detailing of the stone and ironwork. At Packwood, Warwickshire, the cold bath has an ornamental conduit or

32.   Lead fountain wall mask, Packwood House, Warwickshire

springhead, stone steps down to the water and the bath tank itself surrounded by a low wrought iron railing (Plate 31). At Corsham Court, Wiltshire, there is a charming cold bath complete with bath-house, built by Capability Brown in the early 1760's. The pinnacles on the Corsham bath-house were added by Humphry Repton when he was called to Corsham to make further improvements to the estate in 1796.

Formal water features, and fountains in particular, returned to fashion in the mid-19th century following Joseph Paxton's remarkable achievements at Chatsworth and later for the formal gardens adjoining the Crystal Palace at Sydenham. The sixth Duke of Devonshire in 1826 appointed Joseph Paxton, then only twenty-three years of age, as his head gardener at Chatsworth. In those days the position of head gardener to someone as powerful and influential as the Duke of Devonshire would offer great opportunities for most experienced head gardeners; to the young Paxton, then a foreman gardener, it was a remarkable stroke of good fortune. The Duke, however, never had cause to regret the early confidence he had shown in Paxton. Together they developed Chatsworth into one of the wonders of the gardening world. Plant-hunting expeditions were sent to many unexplored parts of the world for new discoveries to fill the fine new glasshouses and the great conservatory that Paxton built at Chatsworth. Under the Duke's patronage, Paxton's interests widened to include civil engineering, architecture, journalism, railway promotion (he was a director of several companies), politics (he became a Liberal member of Parliament for Coventry), and during the Crimean War he organised a civilian engineering corps to improve transport and communications for the troops at the front line. Like so many great Victorians he had started life in quite humble circumstances, but was quick to learn whenever opportunities for education came his way. Most of these opportunities for his education came from the Duke, who took Paxton on extensive continental tours. The two men became lifelong friends, and although many honours and positions were later bestowed upon Paxton, including knighthood, he remained, with the most able assistance from his wife, head gardener and adviser to the sixth Duke throughout the Duke's lifetime. With the Duke Paxton had seen many grand water gardens and fountains on their continental travels, which made the two men determined to make an even grander fountain for Chatsworth. The hillside and its plateau at Chatsworth had for years provided the water for the great cascade and other water features in the gardens, and this same natural advantage was made use of again in Paxton's scheme for the new fountain. To provide the necessary head of water a new reservoir, with a

circumference of nearly three-quarters of a mile, was dug at the top of the hill. By 1843, the reservoir and all the necessary plumbing works were completed, and the fountain given the name of Emperor Fountain after Czar Nicholas of Russia in whose honour it was to have first spouted, when the Emperor visited Chatsworth. Unfortunately the Czar was unable to make the visit from London and had instead to be entertained at Chiswick House, the then London home of the Duke of Devonshire. But the fountain was not a disappointment, for on a still Derbyshire day it could throw a jet of water 290 feet into the air, and was then the highest fountain in the world. The Chatsworth gardeners were justifiably proud of their many record-shattering achievements in the fields of gardening, building, and engineering.

Many of Paxton's layouts owed much to the Italian Renaissance garden; a style he helped to popularise in England in the mid 19th century. After the enormous success of Paxton's 1851 Great Exhibition building in Hyde Park it was decided to re-erect and enlarge the building in a new setting at Sydenham in South London. The formal grounds adjoining the building—soon to be known as the Crystal Palace—were laid out in an Italianate style. For these formal gardens Paxton had built 12,000 fountain jets which when turned on used 120,000 gallons of water per minute. These gardens also contained cast iron water temples, cascades and twin formal lakes where fountains shot water some 250 feet into the air. The Crystal Palace, together with its gardens and park played a big part in the social and educational life of Victorian Londoners, and in garden design produced a

Fig. 65. Cast iron fountain, from Messrs. Boulton and Paul's catalogue of 1896

strong following for the Italian-styled garden and the use again of formal water features and fountains in particular.

The popularity for formal Italian-styled gardens in Britain in the 19th century was not confined to the grounds of the Crystal Palace or the grandiose formal additions to the gardens for such places as Harewood House, Yorkshire, Holkham Hall, Norfolk, and Trentham, Staffordshire. The vogue spread to the market for mass-produced garden ornament. Fountains were designed and produced in a wide range of materials such as cast iron, marble, stone, cast stone, terracotta, lead, bronze, and porcelain. Mass production meant very low costs and soon no owner of an ornamental garden needed to be without a fountain of some sort. The cast iron fountain listed in the 1896 catalogue of Messrs. Boulton and Paul,[1] cost only £4 10s. with a small extra charge for the ground basin (Fig. 65). For the conservatory, less sturdy materials than cast iron were used for the fountain, such as terracotta, porcelain (Fig. 66), and even glass. Whilst some more impecunious owners made their own fountains from unwanted materials, which were discreetly hidden beneath a rustic-looking exterior coating of cement and powdered glass.

Since the 19th-century revival of the use of fountains they have been used as ornaments in gardens, courtyards, and in civic centres. There has not been any one decade especially noted for

Fig. 66. Porcelain fountain for the conservatory, manufactured by John Ridgeway and Co., from the 1851 Great Exhibition catalogue

fountain building, but simply that for the past 170 years they have been in favour as special ornaments for as wide a field as garden

[1] Messrs. Boulton and Paul no longer manufacture garden ornament.

fountains which made a special note of their successful and less successful points, would provide invaluable guidance to many designers about to construct a fountain for the first and probably the last time in their lives. As a general rule fountains need to give a vigorous display in civic centres and similar situations that are bustling with life, otherwise they are hardly noticed. Whilst for small gardens and enclosed courtyards, a very simple jet of water will be most telling but in no way unduly disturbing to the tranquillity to be enjoyed in such a place. Fine jets that create a spray of water can in exposed positions easily have much of the cities to office courtyards. One result has been that no one person has spent a lifetime designing water features. A survey of existing

33. Cast iron pump, Chipping Campden, Gloucestershire

spray carried considerable distances and so cause a great number of unforeseen hazards. A column of water issuing from a large-diameter pipe is less likely to produce a spray hazard and is therefore more suitable for exposed positions. Besides the visual delights to be enjoyed from water in a garden the sound of it is an important part of the pleasure to be derived from fountains. The sound can vary from a heavy thunderous roar to a light tinkle from a small jet spilling into a cistern. The slapping noise of a good jet of water falling on to stonework can also be most effective. This arrangement has been used in the new fountains in Russell Square, London. Here the *bason* has no depth, so that the falling jet of water hits directly on to the stonework and then flows by a gentle fall to the edge of the *bason* back to the pumping mechanism.

Gravity, when this force can be readily made available from an adequate supply, such as a stream or reservoir at a higher level, provides the simplest force to maintain. Without a head of water, some form of pumping mechanism will be required. Electric pumps are mostly employed today, and these if well constructed will give a long period of service.

Sir Edwin Lutyens (1869-1944), was particularly fond of providing water gardens in his schemes. They were always formal in design and often incorporated a dipping well, which was fed from a wall-mask fountain. The dipping tank in turn supplied a flow of water to a lily tank or a formal rill, and further pools at lower levels in the garden. The Lutyens dipping well (Fig. 67) was a most pleasing garden feature. The dipping well consisted of a circular pool which was half vaulted over beneath a terrace. On the underside of the vaulting when the sun was shining, the water would produce a fascinating ripple of reflections. The jet of water falling into the dipping well from the wall mask keeps the water surface in constant motion and so enlivens the reflections on the vaulting above. Lutyens used this device in his designs for the gardens at the Deanery, Sonning, Berkshire, Hestercombe, Somerset, and Abbotswood, Gloucestershire.

Wall fountains mostly consist of a face mask, often cast in lead, with a small pipe for the jet protruding from the mouth. A head of a lion is the most popular design (Plate 32) and many examples of this can be seen in English gardens. Other popular faces for fountain wall masks are heads of Father Thames, cherubs and similar gargoyle figures. New castings in lead of old and modern designs for these masks can still be bought from firms specialising in lead garden ornament.

In recent years there have been a number of most successful

FIG. 67. Dipping well and fountain by Sir Edwin Lutyens, at The Deanery, Sonning, Berkshire

combinations of water *basons*, fountains, and children's paddling pools designed for either children's play parks or for the centrepiece in a small shopping precinct. Like so many original ideas for children's play provision in towns, they have been most developed in Scandinavia. In Stockholm, all the new suburban shopping centres have at least one of these delightful ornamental-cum-children's paddling pools. The pools have to be kept clean and the water passed through a special treatment plant, but this extra provision is well worth while in terms of enjoyment by the local people. When these pools are not full of children enjoying the water and the fountains they look very lacking in life. But once occupied again by small children the pool is a delight for spectators and users alike. Such a happy combination of use and visual delight for ornamental pools in urban areas should be more often the aim of designers of fountains for city open spaces and precincts in Britain. Especially important is this today, now that we have polluted most of the streams and rivers in and around our towns and cities, which once were safe for paddling and generally messing about in by children.

During the 17th and 18th centuries lead cisterns were commonly employed to collect and store rain water for town and country houses. They were usually richly decorated in panels and friezes, often with heraldic motifs. With many of them the date of manufacture was cast as a part of the decoration: the most common dates being 18th-century ones. In shape the lead cistern is generally rectangular (Fig. 52), but there are also a few circular ones. The leadwork over the years has acquired a white patina, which together with the appropriateness of lead and their pleasing decoration makes them welcome ornaments in the garden or courtyard. Not that their use need be confined to decoration, for a cistern can still be put to use for collecting rain water for later use in the garden or as dipping tanks. Since the 18th century rain water cisterns have been constructed in a variety of less expensive materials, such as cast iron, slate, stone, and zinc, but rarely are they so attractive or decorated as were the old lead examples. In recent years plastic replicas of lead cisterns have been manufactured, but, like many other replicas, they do not equal the genuine article.

Before the era of piped mains water supply, wells were an important item in a garden. Their importance, especially on the Continent, was emphasised by the building of beautifully carved well-heads. Sometimes these well-heads had a wrought iron

FIG. 68. Italian well-head

crane which supported a windlass with its chain and bucket. Italy, more than any other European country, is the home of finely carved well-heads and many Italian examples were imported into this country for garden ornaments in the 19th century (Fig. 68). In Italy during the Renaissance, some of the leading artists were employed in the making of decorated well-heads, and many superb examples are to be found today in Venice. The design of most of the Italian well-heads consisted

of a circular opening for the well itself, with a square, hexagon-, or octagon-shaped external face. This face would be richly carved or at least finely moulded.

The crane and windlass mechanism for drawing water from a

FIG. 69. Public drinking fountain, erected in 1865, Victoria Tower Gardens, London

well was superseded by the pump. Many of these early pumps are now preserved or sought after as ornaments for the garden. The old weighted handle type of pump, which, with its sweeping action, if worked with considerable energy gave a constant stream of water, was usually encased in a brick or stone pier. At the foot of the pump there was a trough which when filled would act as a dipping tank for the garden. 19th-century cast iron pumps were usually most elegant in appearance, especially an important pump which served a whole community (Plate 33).

The heavy and cupola-like lid on the top of these pumps was designed to trap as much air as possible and so improve the insulation against frost penetration.

The second half of the 19th century saw the creation of hundreds of public parks and gardens for the urban population of Britain. Their provision arose from the needs of public health and one of the most common and often very striking ornaments in the public parks of the more densely populated areas was the public drinking fountain. Most of the drinking fountains were provided through the agency of the Metropolitan Drinking Fountain and Cattle Trough Association, which was formed in 1859. Before the provision of a local drinking fountain the crowded urban population had to rely on wells which were all too often affected by the polluted subsoil which had been fouled by sewage and too many decomposing bodies. The outbreaks of cholera in 1848-9 and 1853-4 were largely due to the polluted state of the water supplies. Only beer and gin were safe from waterborne diseases. Even in rural areas where no river or spring existed and before many wells had been dug, drinking water in a dry summer could be very unpleasant if not unhygienic. As late

34. The grotto, Woburn Abbey, Bedfordshire

as 1860, some villages during a drought had to depend on muddy water from a pond as the sole source of drinking water. The Metropolitan Drinking Fountain and Cattle Trough Association set about remedying this dreadful situation by the erection of drinking fountains which were to be supplied with clean mains water. Over two thousand public drinking fountains were erected by the Association, of which a great many were sited in the new public parks. Many were a gift by one individual, who, besides showing a fine act of public philanthropy also wished it to be something of a monument to himself or his family. Consequently some of the drinking fountains were enormous structures built with the solidity and heaviness that Victorians always seem to find most appropriate for monuments. Any style for the design of monumental public drinking fountains was acceptable, but Victorian Gothic was the favourite, with polished Scottish granite the new and usually favoured material for their construction. The drinking fountain in the Victoria Tower Gardens, London, erected in 1865, through the generosity of Charles Buxton, M.P., is typical of many to be found in parks in Britain (Fig. 69). Occasionally more elegant and certainly less massive structures were erected, such as the Swan Fountain in the Broad Walk, Regent's Park, London, which was erected in 1887 (Fig. 70). In the 1860's the Association extended its work to include the provision of drinking water for animals. Horse and dog troughs were most required in Victorian towns, but today the horse-trough is very rarely needed, and where they remain they are usually given over to growing flowers and providing a reminder of our former dependence on the horse.

FIG. 70.   Swan drinking fountain, erected in 1887, Broad
Walk, Regent's Park, London

Chapter Six

GATES AND GATEWAYS

Gatehouses; arched gateways; clair-voyées and decorated iron gates; famous smiths of the late 17th and early 18th century; park gatehouses; cast iron gates; painting of iron and timber gates.

THE entrance to the forecourt of a fortified house in mediaeval times was through a gatehouse or barbican. Besides serving to emphasise the point of entry to the grounds surrounding the house, the gatehouse was also a strong point in the surrounding defensive wall. The gatehouse gave the defenders more advantage points from which to combat assailants and would house the mechanism for the drawbridge when the defences included a moat. Long after the need for such defences, the gatehouse continued to be built as the normal entrance to the garden and forecourt of an important country gentleman's seat.

During the great house-building era in Tudor times, gatehouses were still built at the entrance to the forecourt, but from a military point of view they were outdated and were made to look more impressive than they were in reality. One of the best surviving examples of a gatehouse from this period is the one at Charlecote Park, Warwickshire (background of Plate 19). The Charlecote gatehouse was built in the first half of the 16th century and has been attributed to John of Padua. The red brickwork has now mellowed to a beautiful colour and texture. The top of the building has a fine stone balustrading and twin octagonal towers, with ogival shaped cupolas. The archway has stone vaulting more Gothic than Renaissance in style, and some Italian-looking shell-headed alcoves. The interior of this two-

storeyed gatehouse has recently been restored and redecorated through the benevolence of an American visitor.

Gatehouses built to look like a part of a defence system continued to be built up till the 17th century. One of the most charming garden gatehouses to be built in the 17th century is the one at Lanhydrock House, Cornwall (Plate 35), which is equipped with a heavy timber-and-iron door and anachronistic battlements capped with numbers of pinnacles. The Lanhydrock gatehouse, which is built in stone, was begun in 1636, but was not completed until 1651. At that time the forecourt was enclosed by a high wall, which in the 18th century was removed. The present low battlemented wall with its obelisk-like pinnacles (Plate 35) matching with those on the gatehouse were added in 1857 when the delightful formal gardens were laid out in the front of the house.

Gradually the desire to build semi-defensive looking gatehouses diminished, and the simpler arched gateway in the wall was felt to be sufficient. The arched forecourt gateways at Holdenby, Northamptonshire (Fig. 71) built in 1583 are typical of this period, and show also the increasing influence of the Renaissance on garden architecture. By the 17th century, architects no longer considered it necessary always to have such a solid-looking defensive wall to enclose the forecourt and garden. With smaller

FIG. 71.   16th-century arched gateway, Holdenby, Northamptonshire

A *clair-voyée* consisted of panels or grilles of ironwork supported between piers of iron, brick, or stone.   Often a *clair-voyée* would be placed at the end of a formal vista in the garden and so give a view of the outside landscape.   *Clair-voyées* and wrought iron gates were a common feature of the Dutch garden that became so popular in England after William and Mary were crowned in 1689.

It was from the Netherlands that a Huguenot refugee named Jean Tijou came to England and started the golden age of English decorative ironwork.   Tijou introduced *repoussé* work—decorating sheet metal with embossing from blows directed through punches—into England, and his work in this branch of ironwork has never been surpassed.   Before Tijou, smiths had worked at making essentially utilitarian and ordnance ironwork, for the community, and only rarely had they been called upon to design purely decorative ironwork.   Because the smith in the past had been the maker of tools and weapons for the community he had been treated as a most important person.   In Anglo-Saxon times 'he was treated as an officer of the highest rank, and awarded the first place in precedence.   After him ranked the maker of mead, and then the physician'.[1]   With Tijou and his followers, the

FIG. 72.   17th-century gate piers, Ashby St. Ledgers, Northamptonshire

walls the entrance was marked by stone or brick piers, which also supported the gates.   These piers would sometimes have beautifully carved cockle-shell niches (Fig. 72) which it is thought were designed for strangers to sit in whilst awaiting admission to the house.   Surmounting the piers would be some carved decoration either in the form of the owner's heraldic charges (Plate 36) or stone balls.

Gates were now designed less for defensive purposes and more as decoration, which meant that the gate need no longer be of solid timber reinforced by ironwork, but could be a grille of iron bars and scrolls.   This type of gate gave a welcoming view of the garden and house to the visitor or passer-by, but at the same time would exclude unwanted animals.   To keep out small animals an additional row of short bars, known as dog bars, was added to the bottom of gates.   The decorative wrought iron gate could also have its own arch of iron work over the gate itself.   This arch is known as the overthrow which in the 17th and 18th centuries often contained the arms of the owner in some form of wrought or *repoussé* ironwork.   Sometimes the overthrow was thoughtfully hinged to allow the passage of tall objects.

The work of the blacksmith in the 17th century extended beyond the entrance to the garden wall itself, when iron screens known as *clair-voyées* replaced parts of the brick or stone walling.

smith became an artist and craftsman and less of a manufacturer of essential tools and weapons.

Some of Tijou's finest surviving work is at Hampton Court In the fountain garden there is a *clair-voyée* or screen decorated

[1] Samuel Smiles in *Industrial Biography—Workers and Tool Makers*, 1863.

with heraldic emblems, acanthus leaves, and surmounted by masks, which is regarded by many people as his finest work. In the Privy Garden at Hampton Court, adjoining the Barge Walk and the river Thames, is the magnificent Tijou screen, consisting of wrought iron gates or panels, ten feet six inches high. Tijou's motifs for his *repoussé* work were usually masks, eagle heads, and acanthus and bay leaves. His overthrows to the gates often incorporated a monogram made from bar iron. Tijou's work was not confined to gardens, for at such important houses as Hampton Court, and Chatsworth he was responsible for the

design and execution of a number of fine staircases, and for St. Paul's Cathedral he made the sanctuary screen.

After Tijou left England in 1712, a number of now famous smiths continued to maintain his high standard of design and craftsmanship in this country. One of his followers was Robert Bakewell of Derby, whose most spectacular work is the iron arbour known as 'The Birdcage' in the garden of Melbourne Hall, Derbyshire. This magnificent iron arbour was restored in 1958 by the Cambridge firm of George Lister and Sons Ltd. Working at the same time as Bakewell were the Welsh smiths, the brothers

35.   17th-century gatehouse, Lanhydrock House, Cornwall

Robert and Thomas Davies of Wrexham, whose work most resembled that of Tijou, containing as it does both bar and elaborate *repoussé* work. The magnificent iron gates and *clair-voyée* at Chirk Castle, near Llangollen, Denbighshire, were made by the Davies brothers in 1719. There is also an equally splendid screen and gates by these two brothers at Leeswood Hall, Mold, Flintshire, which is some 100 feet in length. Much of the work of Robert and Thomas Davies resembled that of Jean Tijou, and it is probable that the brothers had access to Tijou's book of designs which was published in 1700.

Another great smith making gates and screens at this time was Thomas Robinson of Hyde Park Corner, who, although much less influenced by Tijou, produced some of the finest English decorative ironwork. Robinson's style was less ornate than Tijou's and contained little *repoussé* work. The success of his designs depended on good proportion and the simple elegance of his bar work. His gate and screen to the garden at New College, Oxford, made in 1711, are considered by many to be the most beautiful gateway and screen in Britain. The gate incorporates the founder's arms and motto 'Manners Makyth Man'. The

36. Entrance gates and gate piers, Charlecote Park, Warwickshire

37. Early 18th-century gateway with wrought iron overthrow, Packwood House, Warwickshire

screen and gateway together are some 130 feet in length.

Other famous smiths of this period were William Edney of Bristol who worked mostly in the south and south-west of England; George Buncker who is reputed to have made the elegant gates at Dulwich College, and the Paris family of Warwick. This Golden Age of English ironwork started in about 1690 and lasted until the middle of the 18th century (Plate 37). By the 1740's formal gardens were completely out of fashion, and in many cases destroyed in the making of picturesque landscapes about most country seats of importance. Also by the middle of the 18th century, architects such as Robert Adam were designing ironwork in much more detail, which in time deprived the smith of the ability to produce original work, and so contributed to the decline of the craft.

For the entrance to the picturesque park a new type of gatehouse was built. These gatehouses were in no way a part of a defensive system as they had been in mediaeval times, but were designed simply to give an important appearance to the carriage drive entrance to the park. The park gatehouse would contain one or two dwellings whose occupants were given the duty of opening and closing the gates for the owner of the estate.

In the 19th century many gatehouses were equipped with mechanisms for operating the gates from within the gatehouses themselves. In the 18th century the design of the park gatehouse was invariably classical, but by the end of the century and throughout the 19th century their design became romantic, reflecting the type of countryside they were built in or the taste of the owner (Plate 38).

A revival in the use of ironwork for garden decoration came during the Regency period. Garden designers such as Humphry Repton used iron, copper sheeting, and canvas to form tent-like structures to act as shelters in the newly restored flower gardens. Some of these structures were adapted to form typical features of the Regency house, notably balconies, verandahs, porches, and conservatories. Usually the ironwork was designed in restrained and elegant patterns. It was during this period that cast iron became more used for all forms of garden ornament, including gates and railings, and largely took the place of wrought iron. When the castings were made to imitate wrought work the resultant gate or railing was usually coarse and unattractive. But when the design respected the nature of a cast material, especially its potential robust and solid-looking qualities, then the cast ironwork could have a fine quality of its own. Cast iron gates were also cheaper to manufacture and usually more resistant to weathering, especially in salt-laden atmospheres. Solid-looking cast iron

38.   19th-century gate lodge, Batsford Park, Gloucestershire

gateposts with robust fluting and capped by a sturdy finial were particularly successful.

The Gothic revival in architecture during Victoria's reign, brought about a demand for sham mediaeval ironwork, most frequently executed in cast iron.   The leader of this revival was the architect Augustus Pugin (1812-1852).   Pugin advised Sir Charles Barry on the metalwork for the Palace of Westminster, and many of the churches and colleges built during Pugin's life had iron gates and grilles cast with mediaeval motifs.

The *Art Nouveau* movement that started at the end of the 19th century brought about a minor revival in ironwork.   The curving lines of *Art Nouveau* designs were particularly well expressed by the blacksmith's craft, and a number of garden gates and screens were made in this style.

Today, garden gates are designed in a wide variety of materials, including mild steel, which, if it is simply designed and well protected against rusting, is a satisfactory material. The most pathetic, but all too commonly produced, 'iron' gates are those made in mild steel, but bent and feebly twisted to resemble wrought ironwork. Highly decorated wrought iron is of course expensive, but simple and elegant bar work is not nearly so costly

as many people would think, and the result is one that should last for many lifetimes and be in keeping with all styles of architecture.

Timber gates, if made from a good-quality hardwood and well designed, both from an appearance point of view and the practical need to protect the timber from the weather, will last for a surprisingly long period of time (Plate 39).

Iron gates after perhaps two centuries of use and weathering may need some restoration work, but otherwise the only regular attention needed is painting. Painting, if suitable colours are

39.   Timber entrance gates with Cotswold stone gate piers

used, will enhance the beauty of the ironwork as well as help to preserve it from unsightly and destructive rusting. It is disappointing to see so many fine iron gates and railings in famous gardens in Britain being allowed to rust and consequently deteriorate. Often the horticultural care in these gardens is of a high standard, but the almost irreplaceable ironwork is ignored. As a general rule it should be remembered that ironwork against a light background, such as the sky, makes the gates or railings appear in silhouette, and therefore a dark coloured paint is most appropriate. For this situation black or a dark blue-black paint is normally most successful. When ironwork is seen against dark backgrounds of vegetation or buildings, then white can be most pleasing, although if the ironwork is especially intricate it may still be best to paint it black, with perhaps gilding for finials and *repoussé* work. Timber gates are invariably enhanced if painted white with black for any ironwork that is showing. But there will be many instances where the wood should be kept to its natural colour and treated with a non-colouring preservative. It will then appear more in keeping with the surrounding piers and walls, especially if these are composed of mellow brick or stonework.

Chapter Seven

TREILLAGE

Trellis arbours; Elizabethan garden galleries; French treillage; pleaching; Bacon's description of trellis work; Regency treillage; town gardens and treillage; pergolas.

TREILLAGE or trellis work is a very old form of garden ornament. In Britain it was first used to take the place of a wall to enclose the garden. In Tudor times, flower beds were often surrounded by trellis work which was commonly painted in the armorial colours of the owner and which in most cases must have looked rather lurid in association with the flowers.

The earliest type of garden summer-house was a bower or arbour constructed from simple timber trellis work which supported climbing plants and fruit trees. To begin with the arbour was a part of the garden set aside for the growing of herbs, and was enclosed from the rest of the garden by timber trellis or lattice work. The word arbour is said to be derived from the old English *herbere*, meaning a garden for the growing of herbs. Contemporary illustrations of mediaeval gardens nearly always show an arbour enclosing a turf seat, for the trellis work with its vegetation must have provided some very welcome privacy that was not easily to be found elsewhere in the house or garden.

By the 15th century the trellis work of the arbour had developed into galleries or green tunnels that produced something like a cloistered walk round the garden. The reconstructed Elizabethan Knot Garden at New Place, Stratford upon Avon, (Shakespeare's home when he retired) has a timber gallery supporting trained fruit trees, which gives a most excellent idea of

trellis work of this period (Plate 40). During the reign of James I a gallery made from trellis and plants was thought to be an indispensable part of a well laid out pleasure garden.

Towards the end of the 16th century, timber trellised corridors or galleries reached a most elaborate state of design in the great gardens of France. Quite frequently the trellis work surrounded the then developing kitchen gardens or orchard. In France today there are many surviving examples of beautifully kept kitchen and orchard gardens that are enclosed by galleries and arbours of treillage. Du Cerceau was the principal garden designer of the time, and his achievements in trellis work were the envy of many garden owners in England. Important gardens laid out in England soon followed the French mode for elaborate trellis work. Hampton Court, and Thornbury Castle, Gloucestershire, contained trellis galleries, porticoes and 'green halls' on a scale similar to those to be seen on the Continent. It is from this time that the word treillage is used to denote a more refined and architectural use of trellis work.

Less expensive forms of garden galleries were formed by pleaching and training trees into green tunnels. To begin with the trees were trained to a simple timber framework. Trees that were commonly used for pleaching at that time were elm, lime, and hornbeam.

40.   Timber gallery, New Place, Stratford upon Avon

Francis Bacon (1561-1626), frequently mentions 'carpenter's worke' in his description of an ideal garden in his famous essay *Of Gardens.* Bacon's garden was to have three main parts to it, a green or lawn, a heath or natural garden and a main garden. The green was to contain 'two pleasures ... finely shorn grass' and alleys. His instructions for the treatment of either side of the green was 'to plant a covert alley, upon carpenter's work, about twelve foot in height, by which you may go in shade into the garden'. The main garden was to be 'encompassed on all four sides with a stately arched hedge; the arches to be upon pillars of carpenter's work, of some ten foot high and six foot broad: and the spaces between of the same dimension with the breadth of the arch. Over the arches let there be an entire hedge of some four foot high, framed also upon carpenter's work; and upon the upper hedge, over every arch, a little turret with a belly, enough to receive a cage of birds; and over every space, between arches, some other little figure, with broad plates of round colour'd glass, gilt, for the sun to play upon. But this hedge I intend to be raised upon a bank, not steep, but gently slope, of some six foot, set all with flowers. Also, I understand, that this square of the garden should not be the whole breadth of the ground but to leave on either side ground enough for diversity of side alleys; unto which the two covert alleys of the green may deliver you; but there must be no alleys with hedges at either end of this great inclosure; not at the hither end for letting your prospect upon this fair hedge from the green; nor, at the further end, for letting your prospect from the hedge, through the arches, upon the heath.'

In the early part of the 18th century in Britain, most writers on gardening were advocating the use of French-inspired treillage. John James's book *Theory of Gardening,* published in 1709—a translation from a French book—contained designs for trelliswork of a highly architectural nature (Fig. 73). James's book recommended that treillage should be made up from oak strips of one-inch section formed into six- or seven-inch squares fixed by wire, and framed on to iron supports.

Examples of early 18th-century timber treillage in this country have either perished or were destroyed when the French styled garden went out of fashion in Britain by the 1740's. However, the exquisite arbour known as 'The Birdcage' at Melbourne Hall, Derbyshire, constructed in wrought iron (*c.* 1708-11), still survives to give one an idea of the splendours achieved in treillage during this period. It was designed and made by the smith Robert Bakewell who was undoubtedly much influenced by similar arbours made in the more usual timber strips supported on an iron framework. In France the formal garden has never really gone

out of fashion and consequently many examples of fine treillage work still exist there both in pleasure gardens and in kitchen gardens.

Humphry Repton, the Regency landscape gardener, during

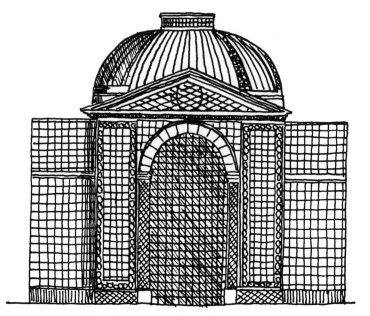

FIG. 73.   A design for trelliswork by John James, from his *Theory of Gardening,* 1709

his latter years used timber and iron trelliswork for his designs for the restored flower garden, which gave rise to a vogue for this ornament both in the garden and for structures attached to the Regency house.

In more recent years, treillage has been used in confined town gardens, in particular in Chelsea and Kensington, to create illusions of vistas and mock prospects. Treillage is particularly suited to the creation of a *trompe l'œil* when attached to the garden wall, and used in conjunction with painted murals, mirrors, and paths laid down with a false perspective.

Pergolas have a similar origin to trellis work, even if their basic construction is different. They have only comparatively recently been introduced into this country from Italy, where they usually supported vines. The purpose of the pergola is to provide a paved walk, which in summer will give a certain amount of cool shade from climbing plants. A pergola is usually constructed from piers of stone, brick or timber which support horizontal timber poles or beams. In Britain the most popular plants for training up and over a pergola are wistaria, roses, ornamental vines, honeysuckle, laburnum, clematis, jasmine, and Russian vine. Sir Edwin Lutyens often made use of pergolas in his garden designs, and greatly helped to popularise them as garden features in English gardens. Architecturally, the pergola can be a most useful element in the formal garden by linking together various parts of the garden, and partially screening less pleasing sections.

BIBLIOGRAPHY

The following are the principal works referred to by the author in the preparation of his manuscript:

ADDISON, JOSEPH: *The Tatler* No. 161, 1710. *The Spectator*, 1712.

ALLEN, B. SPRAGUE: *Tides in English Taste (1619-1800)*, 1937.

BACON, FRANCIS: *Of Gardens*, 1625.

BETJEMAN, JOHN: article on Sezincote, Gloucestershire, in the *Architectural Review*, Vol. 69, 1931.

BLOMFIELD, SIR REGINALD: *The Formal Garden in England*, 1892.

BRIGGS, MARTIN S.: *Men of Taste*, 1947.

Catalogue of Messrs. Boulton and Paul, Ltd., 1896.

Catalogue of The Bo'ness Iron Co. Ltd., 1925.

Catalogue of The Great Exhibition, 1851.

CHADWICK, GEORGE F.: *The Works of Sir Joseph Paxton*, 1961.

CHAMBERS, SIR WILLIAM: *A Dissertation on Oriental Gardening*, 1772.

—— *Designs of Chinese Buildings: Furniture, Dresses, Machines and Utensils from the originals drawn in China by Mr. Chambers, Architect . . . To which is annexed a Description of their temples, houses, gardens, etc.*, 1757.

CHASE, ISOBEL: *Horace Walpole: Gardenist*, 1943.

CLARK, H. F.: *The English Landscape Garden*, 1948.

CLARK, SIR KENNETH: *The Gothic Revival*, 2nd ed., 1928.

CONNOLLY, CYRIL and ZERBE, JEROME: *Les Pavillons, French Pavilions of the Eighteenth Century*, 1964.

CURTIS, CHARLES H. and GIBSON, W.: *The Book of Topiary*, 1904.

DANIELL, THOMAS: *Oriental Scenery*, 1801.

DUTTON, RALF: *The English Garden*, 1936.

EVELYN, SIR JOHN: *The Compleat Garden*, 1693 (English translation of De La Quintinye's work).

FOX, MRS. HELEN: *André le Nôtre, Garden Architect to Kings*, 1962.

GATTY, MRS. ALFRED: *The Book of Sun-Dials*. New and enlarged edition by H. K. F. Gatty and Eleanor Lloyd. With an appendix on the construction of dials by W. Richardson, 1889.

GLOAG, JOHN: *Victorian Comfort, A Social History of Design from 1830-1900*, 1961.

GOTHEIN, MARIE LUISE: *A History of Garden Art* (translated from the German by Mrs. Archer-Hind), 1928.

GREEN, DAVID: *Gardener to Queene Anne—Henry Wise (1653-1738)*, 1956.

GUNNIS, RUPERT: *Dictionary of British Sculptors, 1660-1851*, 1953.

HALFPENNY, WILLIAM: *New Designs for Chinese Temples*, 1750.

HENSLOW, T. GEOFFREY W.: *Garden Architecture*, 1926.

HIBBERD, J. SHIRLEY: *Rustic Adornments for Homes of Taste*, 1856.

—— *The Amateur's Flower Garden*, 1875.

HURTWOOD, LADY ALLEN OF, AND SUSAN JELLICOE: *The New Small Garden*, 1956.

HUSSEY, CHRISTOPHER: *The Picturesque, Studies in a Point of View*, 1927.

JAMES, JOHN: *Theory and Practice of Gardening*, 1712 (a translation from *La Théorie et la Pratique du Jardinage*, published anonymously in France, 1703).

JEKYLL, GERTRUDE, AND HUSSEY, CHRISTOPHER: *Garden Ornament*, 2nd ed., 1927.

JELLICOE, G. A.: *Garden Decoration and Ornament for Smaller Houses*, 1936.

LANGLEY, BATTY: *The City and Country Builder's and Workman's Treasury of Designs, or the art of drawing and working the ornamental parts of architecture . . .*, 1740.

LANGLEY, BATTY & THOMAS: *Ancient Architecture restored and improved by a great variety of grand and useful designs, entirely new, in the Gothic mode for the ornamenting of buildings and gardens*, 1742.

LARWOOD, JACOB: *The Story of the London Parks*, 1881.

LAWSON, WILLIAM: *New Orchard and Garden*, 1618.

LISTER, RAYMOND: *Decorative Wrought Ironwork in Great Britain*, 1957.

—— *Decorative Cast Ironwork in Great Britain*, 1960.

LOUDON, J. C.: *Encyclopaedia of Cottage, Farm and Villa Architecture and Furniture*, 1833.

—— *An Encyclopaedia of Gardening*, 1834.

—— *The Suburban Gardener and Villa Companion*, 1838.

LOUDON, MRS. JANE: *The Ladies' Companion to the Flower Garden*, 1841.

MANWARING, E. W.: *Italian Landscape in Eighteenth Century England*, 1925.

MANWARING, ROBERT: *The Cabinet and Chair-Maker's Real Friend and Companion*, 1765.

MARKHAM, GERVAISE: *Country House* (a re-edited version of Richard Surfleet's translation of Estienne's *Maison Rustique*), 1616.

MARKHAM, VIOLET R.: *Paxton and The Bachelor Duke*, 1935.

MEASON, GILBERT LANG: *On the Landscape Architecture of the Great Painters of Italy*, 1828.

MEYER, FRANZ SALES: *Handbook of Ornament*, first published in 1888, reprinted in 1958.

OVER, CHARLES: *Ornamental Architecture in the Gothic Chinese and Modern Taste, being above fifty intire new designs . . . (Many of which may be executed with roots of trees) for gardens, parks, forests, woods, canals, etc. . . . , 1758.*

PAPWORTH, J. B.: *Rural Residences . . . With Observations on Landscape Gardening, 1818.*

—— *Hints on Ornamental Gardening, 1823.*

PEVSNER, NICHOLAS: *High Victorian Design, 1951.*

PILCHER, DONALD: *The Regency Style, 1946.*

POPE, ALEXANDER: *The Guardian*, No. 173, 1713.

REPTON, HUMPHRY: *Sketches and Hints on Landscape Gardening, 1795.*

—— *Observations on the Theory and Practice of Landscape Gardening, 1803.*

—— *On the Introduction of Indian Architecture and Gardening, 1808.*

—— *Fragments on the Theory and Practice of Landscape Gardening, 1817.*

ROBINSON, WILLIAM: *The Parks, Promenades and Gardens of Paris, Described and Considered in Relation to the Wants of Our Cities, 1869.*

—— *The Wild Garden, 1870.*

—— *The English Flower Garden, 1883.*

ROHDE, ELEANOR SINCLAIR: *Oxford's College Gardens, 1932.*

SHENSTONE, WILLIAM: *The Works in Verse and Prose of William Shenstone,* Dodsley's edition (1764-9).

SHEPHERD and JELLICOE: *Italian Gardens of the Renaissance, 1925.*

SITWELL, EDITH: *Alexander Pope, 1930.*

SMILES, SAMUEL: *Industrial Biography: Workers and Tool Makers, 1863.*

SUMMERSON, JOHN: *John Nash, Architecture to King George IV, 1935.*

SUTTON, THOMAS: *The Daniells, 1954.*

STEWART, CECIL: *Topiary, 1954.*

STROUD, DOROTHY: *Henry Holland, 1745-1806, 1950.*

—— *Capability Brown*, revised edition 1957.

—— *Humphry Repton, 1963.*

THOMPSON, FRANCIS: *A History of Chatsworth, 1949.*

—— *Chatsworth, A Short History, 1951.*

TIPPING, H. AVARY: *English Gardens, 1925.*

TUNNARD, CHRISTOPHER: *Gardens in the Modern Landscape*, 2nd ed., 1948.

WALPOLE, HORACE: *Anecdotes of Painting: With Some Account of the Principal Artists*, a new and revised edition, by Ralf N. Wornum, 1888.

WARD, F. A. B.: *Time Measurement*, Parts I and II, 1958.

WARD-JACKSON, PETER: *English Furntiure Designs of the Eighteenth Century,* 1958.

WEAVER, LAWRENCE. editor: *Engish Furniture Designs of the Eighteenth Century,* 1958.

INDEX

*Illustrations and plates are listed separately at the
beginning of the book and are referred to in the text.*